TABLE OF CONTENTS

LEISURE LIVING GUIDE TO
SLOW COOKING

LL

BOOKS FOR LEISURE LIVING INC.

ISBN number: 0-89165-300-7

Library of Congress Catalog Card Number: 75-20862

INTRODUCTION

The slow-cooking pot which you plug into your electric socket is a sophisticated, modern version of the old way of burying the bean pot in New England for hours and hours of slow cooking without having to keep watch on the pot. The new electric slow-cooking pot frees you from being tied down to the kitchen while your delectable meal is slowly cooking. You may be a working person or attending school, and could prepare the ingredients, place them all in the pot, and go off to your job or your studies. When you come home, you have a hot meal all ready for you. Or, you may have a hobby or you may participate in leisure-time activities which take you away from the kitchen for some time; you can gladly pursue those activities without having to keep watch on the cooking pot. Perhaps you are planning a special dish for a brunch or late breakfast party the next day; you can put the ingredients in the slow-cooking pot, go to bed, and wake up to a cooked meal.

The slow-cooking pot is a saver of precious hours having to be devoted to the kitchen; it is also saving of food costs as the slow-cooking process tenderizes meat and you do not have to always buy the most expensive cuts to produce satisfying dishes. Another cost that is cut down is in electricity, as the slow-cooking pot works on a low wattage. Thus, the savings are in many areas which add to the ease of living.

You do not have to discard your favorite recipes; in the following pages are told the ways you can adapt most of them to your new slow-cooking pot. Also given here are recipes which are suited to the new electrified, slow-cooking methods.

Dorothy Sara
New York, 1975

1

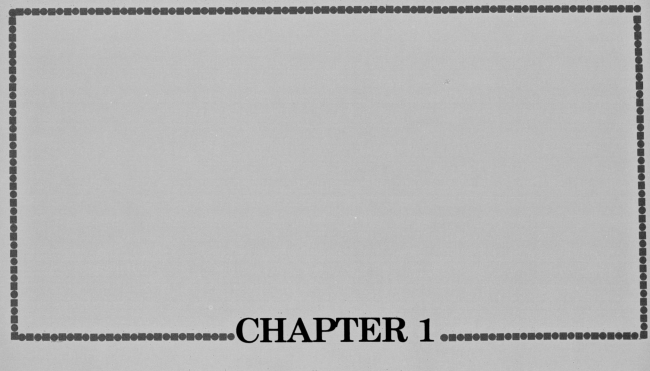

CHAPTER 1

GET ACQUAINTED WITH THE SLOW-COOKING POT

The pot is geared to "low" and "high" with about 200° F. at low, and about 300° F. at high. Usually cooking at "low" takes 8 to 10 hours, and at "high" 3 to 4 hours. You may find it preferable, if you can allot the time, to cook on "low" as it produces tastier meats and it consumes less electricity. If you cannot allow so many hours for the finished meal, you may start on "high" for a short period, then set the pot on "low" for the remainder of the time. Generally 1 hour on "high" is equivalent to 2 to 2½ hours on "low." Using your creativity in the art of cooking, you will be able to devise the time you can allot and the speeds at which to cook, when using recipes you read about or those which are a result of your own experimentation.

OPERATION AND CARE OF POT

After the food is cooked and taken out of the pot, be sure to unplug the cord from the electric outlet. In order to avoid quick temperature changes inside the pot, do not pour in cold water to clean it. Pour in hot, soapy water; this will loosen any food particles. Then with a sponge or rubber spatula or a soft cloth, clean out the inside of the pot. Never use cleaning powders or steel-wool pads or other abrasives.

Do not immerse the pot in water, as that might prove to be an electrical hazard. The outside of the pot should also be cleaned with a soft cloth or sponge and warm, soapy water. Do not use powders or steel-wool pads on the outside either.

When pot is not in use, be sure the cord is not plugged into the electric outlet.

While the food is cooking in the pot, do not touch the hot outside surface of the pot. Use the handles or the knobs.

Warn small children not to handle the pot, especially while food is cooking in it.

If the cord or the outlet is damaged, do not cook in the pot; have the damages repaired first.

Do not use extension cords, but plug directly into the electrical outlet. If necessary to use an extension cord, ask the appliance dealer if its electrical rating matches the rating of the pot.

Make sure the cord does not rest on or touch any hot surface; also the cord should not hang down over the edge of a counter or table, as a person passing by might inadvertently pull that cord and cause damage.

Do not cook outdoors near a barbecue grill or fireplace.

Never place the pot on or in a heated oven, or on a hot electric burner or gas plate.

Never use the pot to store foods in the refrigerator.

Do not use appliances with the slow-cooking pot, unless you check them out with the appliance dealer or the manufacturer. However, you could use a metal trivet or a rack, placed on the bottom of the slow-cooking pot before you put the food into the pot, in cases where you do not want the meat or other food to touch the pot itself and have space for excess fat to drain off. Do not use such rack or trivet as a general procedure; but only in cases where the recipe suggests you do so. Also, you will find some of the recipes instruct that a metal baking pan or mold be used, and in others the use of metal coffee cans is suggested. These cans may come in 1 lb. size or larger, and they serve as good baking receptacles for certain cakes and desserts.

Before you buy any trivet, rack, mold or baking pan to use inside your slow-cooking pot, make sure to measure inside the pot so that you get these "extras" to properly fit and not be too large.

Crock-Pot slow cooker courtesy of Rival Manufacturing Company

CHAPTER 2

COOKING HINTS

It is not necessary to stir food in a slow-cooking pot; however, sometimes when cooking on high heat you may wish to do so. It is not necessary to stir while cooking on low.

Spices and herbs, when added to ingredients in the pot, may result in too strong a flavor in some cases. It is advisable, therefore, to go easy on them (if you want the food to be subtly flavored); this could also apply to onions, garlic, or other high-flavor vegetables. Your own taste buds will tell you the amounts most desirable to use. It may be best to add spices during last hour of cooking.

Slow cooking—gentle cooking—gives a better flavor to foods; also foods are more tender when done in the slow-cooking pot.

As less moisture evaporates in this process of cooking, meats come out tender (so you may find a saving in some of the less expensive cuts).

When combining vegetables and meat in a roast, for instance, the vegetables should be placed at the bottom of the pot; this keeps the vegetables moist, and they should be cut into small pieces or quartered.

Sometimes you may find too much liquid at the end of cooking time. To reduce the liquid, remove the cover from the slow-cooking pot and set it on high for approximately 45 minutes. Another suggestion about too much liquid is that you use half the recommended amount of liquid specified in the conventional recipe.

Some foods do not call for long hours of cooking; for instance, rice, noodles and other pasta, milk, seafood, Chinese vegetables. To get best results, these should be added the last 2 hours when you cook on low, or the last hour when cooking is on high.

If the recipe includes cooked rice or pasta, they should first be cooked according to package directions (not overcooked), and stirred in with the other ingredients. But if the recipe calls for raw rice, then add an extra cup of liquid to one cup of the rice. It is suggested you use long grain converted rice for best results in slow cooking.

You may find that by substituting evaporated milk instead of homogenized milk, especially in slow cooking for 8 hours or so, you will get better results.

It is not absolutely necessary to add water when cooking a roast; but it is suggested that a small amount of liquid be added so it may be used for making tasty gravy. The more fat (marbling) the meat contains, the less liquid need be used.

Gravy can be made in the slow-cooking pot, using whatever recipe you like. When you want a thick gravy, add some minute tapioca to the pot, a short while before the end of the cooking. Thus it will thicken as it cooks. When food is removed from the pot, leave the juices in pot. Make a thin paste of even amounts of flour and water. Add paste to the juices, set on high, cook approximately 15 minutes. (This paste of flour and water can be added just to the juices for a thin gravy, or to the tapioca-cooked-with-juices for a thick gravy.)

It is not usually necessary to brown meat (excepting pork, bacon, lamb, or excessively fatty beef or veal). All you need to do is to trim off any fat which you feel is in excess, then with a towel pat the meat dry, and place it into the pot. But if the meat is excessively fatty and should be browned, do that in your usual way of heating some oil or fat in a skillet, and tossing the pieces of meat in a mixture of flour, salt and pepper, and sautéing the coated meat in the skillet, browning on all sides. Place the browned meat into the slow-cooking pot with all other ingredients.

If you cannot get home in time to turn off the pot, say at the end of 8 or 10 hours, or whatever time you had planned, do not let this be of much concern. The food will not be burned, the liquid will not be drained off, as in the conventional manner of cooking; it will just be cooked a little more and be more tender. However, if you are cooking a pot roast or some other food that has to be sliced, it is not good to overcook it as it becomes too tender for such slicing. If you are not too sure that you can return at a specified time (to coincide with the time you want the cooking to terminate), you should leave the cooking set on low; then, when you come home you can change the setting to high if you want to speed the time. Timing is something you have to decide for yourself, in specific cases—but it is an easy matter to which you can adjust.

Additional use of the slow-cooking pot is that it may act as a buffet server, to keep food warm. Also it could be used as a bun warmer. To reheat foods, all you need to do is to set the pot on low, cover it, and heat for two to four hours.

You will find that some recipes instruct you to use aluminum foil as a cover of the pan or coffee can in which the contents are cooking inside the slow-cooking pot. The foil is to be cut to allow for 1 inch or more to be bent down all around the top of the can; then tied down with a string to keep in place. The purpose of this is to get quicker cooking. In some recipes you will find that it is best to put a paper towel over the top of the container which is inside the slow-cooking pot. It is best not to experiment with the use of foil or towel as extra cover, unless the recipe calls for doing so.

When the recipe includes frozen foods, do not place the food into the slow-cooking pot directly from the opened package. First thaw it, as you would in any conventional type of cooking. Some recipes call for partially-thawed foods; but if they do not explicitly say so it is best to do a more complete thawing.

If you live in a high altitude, where you find the timing in recipes for conventional cooking takes longer than in low-altitude areas, you will need to allow for more cooking time in some cases (than the recipe suggests). If this is so, when cooking a certain food for the first time (which needs longer time in high altitudes) it is suggested that you make notes on the recipe as to length of time required, so the next time you repeat this same dish you will know how to proceed.

CHAPTER 3

ADAPTING CONVENTIONAL RECIPES

In the following chapters are given recipes which are devised for slow-cooking, one-step methods. However, you may have favorite recipes which you could adapt to this slow method, by these general rules (and by creating your own ways, too).

First, you may have to figure out the cooking time, and it is recommended that you follow this guide:

Your recipe	*Slow-cooking pot*
15 to 30 minutes	1½ to 2½ hours on high
	4 to 8 hours on low
35 to 45 minutes	3 to 4 hours on high
	6 to 10 hours on low
50 minutes to 3 hours	4 to 6 hours on high
	8 to 18 hours on low

Not all conventional recipes can be adapted to slow-cooking method, such as salads, cold soups, and foods which need to be broiled or deep-fried.

As told in previous chapter, spices and herbs and such standard seasonings as salt and pepper may need to be reduced in amount. It is best to add seasonings (especially the ground ones, and not the fresh herbs) during the last hour of cooking. Your own taste will guide you in the amount of seasonings and herbs which blends best with the recipe in the slow-cooking pot.

If a recipe calls for the cooked food to be served on a bed of cooked rice, noodles or other pasta, or mashed or french-fried potatoes, these should be cooked separately and be ready when the food from the pot is to be served. If time is precious to you, as a matter of convenience you might use the "instant" rice or the "powdered" potatoes which can be instanteously prepared by the addition of boiling water, as directed on the boxes in which they are packed.

If a recipe calls for a topping of crisp bacon bits, bread crumbs, grated cheese or tomato wedges, add these at the very end of cooking time, just before the food is served.

When the food is to be served with a topping of a pie crust, or a biscuit, or mashed potatoes, prepare these separately before the end of the cooking time. Then remove the food, put it into a baking dish, add the topping, and proceed to "brown" the topping in the regular oven as called for in a conventional recipe.

If you have some broth or gravy in the slow-cooking pot and want to cook dumplings (according to your favorite recipe), set the cooker on high, and when the liquid simmers drop the dumpling mixture into it by spoonfuls. Cover pot and cook for approximately 30 minutes.

The use of milk was mentioned in preceding chapter; it is well to add here that milk, cream and sour cream do not fare too well in long hours of cooking, so it is best to add them during the last hour of cooking. Sometimes, when a recipe calls for milk or cream, you could substitute canned condensed soup which can be cooked for a long time. If you use a recipe which does not include any liquid other than milk or cream, to start off the cooking you should add 1 or 2 cups of water (dependent on the amount of food in the recipe) and just before serving add the milk or cream and heat it with the rest of the ingredients.

In making soup in the slow-cooking pot, you may be following a conventional recipe which calls for 2 or more quarts of water. In such case, put the soup ingredients into the pot, but add only enough water to cover the food, because liquid does not boil away in the slow-cooking pot. If you want a thinner soup, add more liquid shortly before serving time.

Stews do not need large amounts of water when made in the slow-cooking pot. One cup of liquid is usually sufficient. Just before removing from pot for serving, you may want to taste the stew and perhaps add a bouillon cube to it for additional flavor.

When cheese is included in a recipe, it may be best to use processed cheeses, such as American cheese or prepared cheese spreads, rather than the sharper-tasting cheddar cheese. However, your own taste preference will determine which to use.

The recipes suggested in this book are for 4 to 6 servings. If you want less or more, proportionately alter the amounts of the ingredients.

The following tables of standard equivalents apply to the recipes given in this book:

EQUIVALENT MEASURES

3 teaspoons	= 1 tablespoon
4 tablespons	= ¼ cup
16 tablespons	= 1 cup
2 cups	= 1 pint
2 pints	= 1 quart
4 quarts	= 1 gallon
2 tablespoons	= 1 fluid ounce
1 cup	= 8 fluid ounces
16 ounces	= 1 pound

EQUIVALENT AMOUNTS

1 cup uncooked rice	= 3 cups cooked rice
1 pound butter or margarine	= 2 cups
1 stick butter (¼ pound)	= ½ cup
1 pound granulated sugar	= 2 cups
1 pound brown sugar	= 2¼ cups
1 pound powdered sugar	= 3½ cups
1 pound all-purpose flour	= 4½ cups, sifted
1 pound cheese	= 4½ cups, grated
1 square chocolate	= 1 ounce
1 pound cocoa	= 4 cups
1 pound macaroni	= 4 cups—10 cups cooked
1 medium onion	= ½ cup chopped
1 cup uncooked cornmeal	= 4 cups cooked mush
1 pound shortening	= 2 cups
1 pound raisins, seedless	= 3¼ cups
1 pound walnuts in shell yields	½ pound nuts

CHAPTER 4

BEEF RECIPES

POT ROAST

3 to 4 lbs. pot roast (or rump)
2 Tbsp shortening
1 tsp salt
¼ tsp pepper
3 medium potatoes, peeled, halved
　3 medium carrots, peeled, quartered
2 medium onions, peeled, halved
½ cup water or beef broth

Brown meat on both sides in hot shortening in skillet. Into bottom of the slow-cooking pot place half the vegetables. Salt and pepper the meat. Put meat atop vegetables in pot; add remaining vegetables and the liquid. Cook on low 10 to 12 hours, or on high 5 to 6 hours.

STEAK ROULADE

2 thin round steaks (1½ lbs. each)
2 tsp salt
2 tsp pepper
¾ cup chopped onion
¾ cup chopped bacon
¼ cup water

Trim fat off steaks. Season with salt and pepper. Mix onion and bacon, spread over each steak. Roll steaks (as you'd do for a jelly roll, tie rolls tightly in several places with a string. Put steaks into slow-cooking pot. Add the water. Cover pot. Cook on low for 8 hours. If you want to serve this with gravy, remove meat when done, and thicken liquid with a mixture of flour and water, and cook it in pot set at high for 15 minutes.

CHILI BEEF

2 lbs. boneless round steak
1 clove garlic, peeled, minced
½ tsp salt
¼ tsp pepper
1 Tbsp chili powder
1 Tbsp prepared mustard
1 onion, peeled, chopped
1 16-oz. can tomatoes, mashed
1 beef bouillon cube, crumbled
1 16-oz. can kidney beans,
    drained
Cooked rice

In a bowl mix the garlic, salt, pepper, chili powder and mustard. Spread mixture over meat. Cut meat into strips. Place meat in slow-cooking pot. In a bowl mix the onion, tomatoes and bouillon cube. Pour mixture into pot. Cover pot. Cook on low 6 to 8 hours, or on high 3 to 4 hours. Add beans to pot. Cover pot. Cook on high 30 minutes. Serve over cooked rice, which has separately been prepared.

CORNED BEEF, GLAZED

4 lbs. corned beef
Water
2 Tbsp prepared horseradish
2 Tbsp prepared mustard
¼ cup molasses
2 Tbsp wine vinegar

Put beef in slow-cooking pot. Pour in water to cover meat. Cover pot. Cook on low 10 to 12 hours, or on high 5 to 6 hours. In a bowl mix all other ingredients. Remove meat from pot. Brush the mixture all over the meat's surface. Put meat in a baking pan in the oven for 15 minutes, or until it is brown. During the browning process in oven, spread sauce over the meat's surface.

BASIC ROAST BEEF

3 to 4 lbs. pot roast, rump roast
    or brisket
Salt, pepper, or other desired
    seasonings

Season meat to your taste. Place meat in slow-cooking pot. Do not add any liquid. Cover pot. Cook on low 10 to 12 hours, or on high 4 to 5 hours.

POT ROAST WITH VEGETABLES

3 to 4 lbs. pot roast, rump roast
   or brisket
3 medium potatoes, peeled,
   sliced
1 large onion, peeled, sliced
3 medium carrots, peeled, sliced
½ cup water or beef broth
Salt and pepper, to taste

Place vegetables in slow-cooking pot. Salt and pepper meat, put meat into pot. Add liquid. Cover pot. Cook on low 10 to 12 hours, or on high 4 to 5 hours.

BEEF BURGUNDY

1½ lbs. boneless chuck, cut into
   2-inch pieces
¾ cup dry red wine
1 tsp salt
⅛ tsp pepper
½ tsp paprika
½ tsp crumbled leaf marjoram
   (optional)
1 large onion, peeled, sliced
½ lb. fresh small mushrooms (or
   if large, chopped)
1 large green pepper, seeded, cut
   into strips
Cooked rice or noodles

Brown pieces of beef in skillet, as told in Chapter 2. Place meat in slow-cooking pot. Drain fat from skillet. Pour wine into skillet, stir into the brown leavings; pour this over the meat. Sprinkle meat with salt, pepper, paprika and marjoram. Add onions, mushrooms, green peppers. Stir all to mix. Cover pot. Cook on low 10 to 12 hours, or on high 4 to 5 hours. Prepare separately boiled rice or noodles, and dish the beef over this.

BEEF SAUERBRATEN

3 lbs. rump pot roast
1½ tsp salt
½ tsp pepper
1½ cups onions, peeled, chopped
1¼ cups (or 10½ oz. can) beef
  broth
1 cup red wine vinegar
1 bay leaf (optional)
6 ginger snaps, crushed
Boiled red cabbage and potatoes

Rub salt and pepper over entire surface of meat. Place in slow-cooking pot with onions, broth, vinegar and bay leaf. Cover pot. Let meat marinate 3 to 4 hours (or overnight). Occasionally turn the meat to absorb the marinate liquid. To start cooking, place meat in slow-cooking pot. Cover pot. Cook on low for 8 hours. Remove meat to a serving platter. Slice it, and keep warm. Skim the fat from liquid in pot. In a saucepan, on top of your stove, place the crushed ginger snaps and slowly pour in the pot liquor. Stir and heat until gravy thickens and bubbles; you may add more salt and pepper if you desire. When serving the meat slices, pour the hot gravy over them. This dish is usually accompanied by boiled red cabbage and boiled potatoes, which you have prepared separately and are ready for serving when the sauerbraten is taken from the slow-cooking pot.

BARBECUED MEAT

Choose short ribs or whatever cut of beef you want, and cut into serving pieces, and in any amount you prefer. Season the pieces of meat with salt, pepper, garlic salt, or whatever other seasonings your taste dictates. Cover each piece with barbecue sauce (which, for easy cooking, you can buy prepared). Do not add any water. Place the meat in slow-cooking pot. Cook on low for 8 to 10 hours, or on high 4 to 6 hours. If you want an extra flavor, during the last ½ hour of cooking you could add a small can of drained pineapple chunks.

BRAISED SHORT RIBS

2½ lbs. short ribs, cut in pieces
¾ tsp salt
¼ tsp pepper
¾ cup flour
1½ Tbsp oil
1 large onion, peeled, sliced
¾ cup beef broth
¼ tsp whole allspice (optional)
1 bay leaf (optional)

Mix salt, pepper and flour, and coat the pieces of short ribs in the mixture to coat the meat. Brown in hot oil in a skillet. Place ribs in slow-cooking pot. Add remaining ingredients. Cover pot. Cook on low 8 to 10 hours, or on high 4 to 6 hours. Serve with or without gravy, as desired.

14

TACO SHORT RIBS

4 lbs. short ribs
1 pkg taco seasoning mix
1 10½-oz. can beef consomme
1 green pepper, chopped

In a skillet on top of stove, brown meat. Drain off excess fat. In a bowl mix taco seasoning and consomme. Add green pepper to bowl. Put short ribs in slow-cooking pot. Pour sauce into pot. Cover pot. Cook on low 6 to 8 hours, or on high 3 to 4 hours.

SHORT RIBS WITH CHILI

3 lbs. short ribs, cut into pieces
2 garlic cloves, peeled, chopped
2 tsp chili powder
1 1-lb. can tomatoes
1 tsp salt
⅛ tsp pepper
2 medium onions, peeled, sliced
1 green pepper, seeded, cut into
    squares
1 1-lb. can kidney beans,
    drained
½ tsp. sugar

In a large, heated skillet rub the fatty edge of a short rib over the surface of the pan. Then brown all ribs on all sides, Put browned ribs in slow-cooking pot. In skillet lightly brown the garlic, stir in chili powder, add slightly mashed tomatoes and the juice. Stir to mix. In the slow-cooking pot sprinkle ribs with salt and pepper, add onions and green pepper. Pour tomato mixture over all, and mix by stirring. Cover pot. Cook on low 8 to 10 hours, or on high 4 to 6 hours. About 2 hours before cooking is finished on low, or 1 hour before on high, add kidney beans. Cover. Continue cooking. When serving, put meat and vegetables on platter, and discard bones (from which meat has fallen away) if you desire. Into a bowl place the liquid, skim off fat. If you want to use this as thickened gravy, put the liquid in a saucepot on top of stove and thicken with flour. Or use it just as it is.

BRISKET AND BEER

3½ lbs. brisket, lean
1 onion, peeled, sliced
2 celery stalks, chopped
½ cup chili sauce
1½ tsp salt
¼ tsp pepper
1 bottle beer

Put meat in slow-cooking pot. In a bowl mix the other ingredients, except beer. Into pot put the mixture over the meat. Pour the beer over all. Cover pot. Cook on low 8 to 10 hours, or on high 4 to 5 hours. Place meat on serving platter, and slice it. Serve juice in separate bowl, to pour over slices.

STUFFED PEPPERS WITH CORN

6 green peppers, seeded, cored
½ to ¾ lb. ground beef, lean
1 Tbsp pimiento, chopped
¼ cup onion, chopped fine
1 12-oz. can corn kernels,
   drained
1 tsp salt
1 can condensed cream of
   tomato soup
1 tsp prepared mustard
1 Tbsp Worcestershire sauce

In a bowl mix beef, pimiento, onion, corn and salt. With a spoon, stuff mixture into peppers. Put peppers in slow-cooking pot, standing upright. In a bowl mix the soup, mustard and Worcestershire. Pour mixture into pot. Cover pot. Cook on low 8 to 10 hours, or on high 4 to 5 hours.

MEAT LOAF

2 lbs. chuck, ground
2 eggs, beaten
¾ cup milk
1 tsp salt
½ tsp pepper
3 slices bread, crumbed
½ cup onion, peeled, chopped
¼ cup green pepper, seeded, chopped
¼ cup celery, chopped
½ cup ketchup

In a bowl mix eggs, milk, seasonings and bread crumbs into a soft consistency. Add meat, vegetables and most of the ketchup, and thoroughly mix. Shape the mixture into a loaf. Place it in the slow-cooking pot. Use the rest of the ketchup to spread over the loaf. Cover pot. Cook on low 6 to 8 hours, or on high 3 to 4 hours.

16

BEEF STEW

4 carrots, peeled, sliced
3 potatoes, peeled, cubed
2 lbs. stew meat, cut in cubes
1 cup beef broth
1 tsp salt
1 tsp pepper
1 tsp fine herbs
1 tsp onion powder
1 celery stalk, cut up
1 small can peas, drained (optional)

In the order in which these ingredients are listed, excepting the peas, they should be placed in the slow-cooking pot. Stir a few times. Cover pot. Cook on low 10 to 12 hours, or on high 5 to 6 hours. If desired, at the last ½ hour of cooking the peas may be added.

SWISS STEAK

2 lbs. round steak (¾-inch thick)
Salt and pepper, to taste
1 large onion, peeled, sliced
   thinly
1 8-oz. can tomatoes

Cut meat into serving pieces. Season with salt and pepper. Place meat and onion in slow-cooking pot. Pour tomatoes over them. Cover pot. Cook on low 8 to 10 hours, or on high 4 to 6 hours.

CORNED BEEF AND CABBAGE

3 medium carrots, peeled, cut in
   3-inch pieces
3 to 4 lbs. corned beef brisket
2 to 3 medium onions, peeled,
   quartered
Cabbage, cut in small wedges
1 to 2 cups water

In the order in which the ingredients are listed, put them in slow-cooking pot. Cover pot. Cook on low 10 to 12 hours, or on high 5 to 6 hours. So that the cabbage wedges are well-moistened, uncover pot after 5 to 6 hours on low (or 2 to 3 hours on high) and push the wedges down into the liquid. Cover pot. Continue cooking. You may want to cook corned beef without the vegetables, or you may prefer to substitute other vegetables, or to boil potatoes separately and serve with this dish. But the forgoing ingredients are those usually contained in this meat recipe.

GROUND BEEF AND POTATOES

2½ lbs. ground beef, lean
¼ cup onion, chopped fine
1 tsp salt
½ tsp pepper
1 can condensed tomato soup,
    undiluted
6 medium potatoes, peeled,
    sliced
1 cup light cream

In a skillet, on the oven, brown the meat to remove excess fat. Pour off fat. In a bowl mix the onion, salt, pepper and soup. Put into slow-cooking pot a layer of potato slices, then a layer of meat; then another layer of potatoes and topped with rest of the meat. Pour soup mixture into pot. Cover pot. Cook on low 4 to 6 hours, or on high 2 to 3 hours. Pour cream into pot. Cover pot. Cook on high 15 minutes.

JAPANESE STEAK

2½ lbs. boneless chuck steak, cut
    in thin strips
½ cup soy sauce
1 garlic clove, peeled, minced
2 Tbsp oil
½ Tbsp sugar
1 tsp ginger, ground
1 can beef broth, undiluted
Cooked rice

Put meat strips in slow-cooking pot. In a bowl mix all other ingredients. Pour mixture over meat. Cover pot. Cook on low 6 to 8 hours, or on high 3 to 4 hours. Serve on a bed of cooked rice, which you had separately prepared.

LIVER WITH TOMATOES

2 lbs. sliced liver
4 bacon strips, cut in thirds
1 can stewed tomatoes
½ cup carrot, peeled, chopped
½ cup celery, chopped
1 onion, peeled, sliced
1 tsp salt
⅛ tsp pepper

Put liver in slow-cooking pot. Put bacon strips on top of liver. In a bowl mix other ingredients. Pour mixture into pot. Cover pot. Cook on low 6 to 8 hours, or on high 3 to 4 hours.

STEAK WITH MUSHROOM GRAVY

2½ lbs. round steak
¼ cup water
1 can condensed cream of
  mushroom soup, undiluted
1 pkge. onion soup mix

In a bowl mix ingredients, excepting steak. Cut steak in 6 pieces. Place meat in slow-cooking pot. Pour soup mixture over meat. Cover pot. Cook on low 6 to 8 hours, or on high 3 to 4 hours. Remove meat on serving platter. Pour sauce over steak, when served.

ORIENTAL STEAK

3 lbs. round steak, 1 inch thick,
  cut in cubes
1 garlic clove, peeled, minced
6 small onions, peeled, sliced
6 medium green peppers, seeded, cut in 1-inch squares
1 8-oz. can sliced water chestnuts
1 6-oz. jar sliced mushrooms
⅛ tsp thyme
1 8-oz. can tomato sauce
1 tsp sugar
2 tsp salt
¼ tsp pepper
3 cups cold water
Cooked rice

Courtesy of Planters Peanut Oil

In the order in which the ingredients are listed, excepting the rice, put them in slow-cooking pot. Stir well. Cover pot. Cook on low 8 to 10 hours, or on high 4 to 5 hours. Separately prepare cooked rice, on which the dish is served.

BEEF AND WINE CASSEROLE

2 lbs. chuck or stewing meat, cut
   in 2-inch cubes
1½ cup red wine (Burgundy
   preferred)
 2 10½-oz. cans condensed beef
   consomme
½ tsp salt
¼ tsp pepper
2 medium onions, peeled, sliced
¼ cup fine bread crumbs
¼ cup flour

Put all ingredients, excepting bread crumbs and flour, in slow-cooking pot. Mix crumbs and flour and stir in. Cover pot. Cook on low 8 to 10 hours, or on high 4 to 5 hours.

BRAISED OXTAILS

2 oxtails, cut at joints
¼ cup butter or margarine
Salt and paprika, to taste
2 cups boiling tomato juice or
   beef juice
8 small onions, peeled
½ cup celery, diced
½ cup carrots, peeled, diced
Cooked noodles

In a skillet brown the oxtails in butter or margarine. Season with salt and paprika. Add tomato juice or broth. Let this cool. Put into slow-cooking pot, add the vegetables, but do not add noodles. Cover pot. Cook on low 10 to 12 hours, or on high 5 to 6 hours. When cooked, skim off fat. If desired, thicken stock with flour. Separately prepare cooked noodles, and serve oxtails and vegetables over them.

BEEF TONGUE

1 tongue (smoked or fresh)
2 Tbsp salt
1½ cups water
1 bay leaf
2 medium onions, peeled,
   quartered
6 peppercorns
If using smoked tongue, delete salt.

Wash tongue. Put all in pot. Cover pot. Cook on low 8 to 10 hours, or on high 4 to 5 hours. When done, drain liquid, discard onions and seasonings. Tongue may be served hot or cold with whatever accompaniments are desired.

HUNGARIAN GOULASH

2 lbs. round steak, cut in ½-inch
  cubes
1 cup onions, peeled, chopped
1 garlic clove, peeled, minced
2 Tbsp flour
1 tsp salt
½ tsp pepper
1 Tbsp paprika
¼ tsp dried, crushed thyme
1 bay leaf
1 12-oz. can tomatoes
1 cup sour cream
Cooked noodles

Put meat, onion and garlic in slow-cooking pot. Stir in the flour to coat the steak cubes. Add all ingredients, excepting sour cream. Stir to mix well. Cover pot. Cook on low 7 to 10 hours, or on high 5 to 6 hours. Add sour cream 30 minutes before cooking is finished, stirring the cream thoroughly. Serve on a bed of cooked noodles, which you have separately prepared.

FLANK STEAK CASSEROLE

2 flank steaks
2 Tbsp lemon juice
1 Tbsp salt
Dash of pepper
Dash of nutmeg (optional)
Dash of cloves (optional)
2 tbsp onion, peeled, minced
2 cups bread crumbs
2 cups tomatoes, diced
1 qt tomato juice

With a fork or knife score both sides of steak. Sprinkle with lemon juice and onions. Combine onion, bread crumbs and tomatoes, and spread on steaks. Roll them (like a jelly roll) and fasten with string. Put in slow-cooking pot. Add tomato juice. Cover pot. Cook on low 6 to 8 hours, or on high 3 to 4 hours. You may serve liquid as it is, or else thicken it with flour and water and cook it on high for 15 minutes.

STUFFED CABBAGE

2 medium size cabbages
1½ lbs. beef, ground
2 cups raw rice
2 eggs
1 No. 2½ can sauerkraut
1 onion, peeled, chopped
1 garlic clove, peeled, minced
Salt and pepper, to taste
1 No. 2½ can tomatoes, solid
   pack, whole

Prepare a large pot of boiling water. Remove core from cabbages; put both heads of cabbage into pot of water. When the cabbage is parboiled, remove the leaves from each head. Cut off the top of each leaf (to remove any stiff parts of remaining core), so the leaf is flexible and can be rolled. Mix meat with all other ingredients, excepting tomatoes and sauerkraut. Fill separate leaves with meat mixture, and roll them. Put a layer of tomatoes in slow-cooking pot. Put some cabbage rolls on top, then a layer of sauerkraut. Repeat the layering of tomatoes, cabbage rolls and sauerkraut until all used. Pour over all the juice from tomato can. Cook on low 10 to 12 hours, or on high 5 to 6 hours.

SMOTHERED STEAK

1½ lbs. chuck or round steak, cut
   in strips
⅓ cup flour
½ tsp. salt
¼ tsp pepper
1 large onion, peeled, sliced
1 large green pepper, seeded,
   sliced
1 1-lb. can tomatoes
1 4-oz. can mushrooms, drained
2 Tbsp molasses (optional)
1 10-oz. package frozen string
   beans (optional)
Cooked rice

Place meat, flour, salt and pepper in slow-cooking pot. Stir well so that strips of meat are coated by the mixture. Place all remaining ingredients, excepting rice, in pot. Cover pot. Cook for 1 hour on high; then cook for 8 hours on low. Or cook entirely on high for 5 hours. Serve on cooked rice, which you have separately prepared.

BEEF STROGANOFF

2 lbs. beef, ground, or cut into
   short, narrow strips
2 Tbsp shortening
2 medium onions, peeled,
   chopped
2 garlic cloves, peeled, minced
1 8-oz. can sliced mushrooms,
   drained
¼ tsp salt
¼ tsp pepper
1 cup beef broth
3 Tbsp tomato paste
1½ cups sour cream, blended
   with 4 Tbsp flour
6 Tbsp Burgundy wine (optional)
Cooked noodles or rice

In a skillet melt the shortening, then brown the meat in it. To the skillet add onions, garlic and mushrooms. Stir and sauté until onion is golden brown. Put into slow-cooking pot with other ingredients, excepting noodles or rice. Stir to mix well. Cover pot. Cook on low 6-8 hours. (Because of the low heat, it is all right to add the sour cream with the other ingredients at beginning of cooking.)

Courtesy of The Pan American Coffee Bureau

GROUND BEEF STROGANOFF

1½ lbs. ground beef
3 strips bacon, cut in small
   pieces
1 medium onion, peeled,
   chopped
¼ tsp salt
¼ tsp paprika
1 Tbsp flour
2 Tbsp dry red wine
1 can condensed cream of
   mushroom soup, undiluted
1 cup sour cream
Toasted buns or bread slices

In a skillet, on top of oven, put beef and bacon. Brown them; drain to remove excess fat. Put meat and bacon in slow-cooking pot. Add to pot the onion, salt, paprika, flour and wine. Stir in pot to mix all. Pour wine and soup into pot, mix well. Cover pot. Cook on low 4 to 5 hours, or on high 2 to 2½ hours. Just before serving, add sour cream to pot and stir to mix. Serve over toasted buns.

BEEF WITH ORANGE SAUCE

3 lbs. lean beef, cut in 1-inch
   cubes
1½ tsp salt
¼ tsp pepper
3 10½-oz. cans beef gravy
⅓ cup orange juice
⅓ cup currant jelly
1¼ cups broiled mushrooms, or
   canned
⅓ can pimiento-stuffed olives,
   sliced
2 bay leaves
Cooked rice

Place all ingredients, excepting the rice, into slow-cooking pot. Stir well to mix. Cover pot. Cook on low 8 to 10 hours, or on high 4 to 5 hours. Serve on cooked rice, which you have prepared separately.

SLOPPY JOES

3 lbs. ground meat
2 medium onions, peeled, chopped fine
1 green pepper, seeded, chopped (optional)
2 8-oz. cans tomato sauce
1 cup water
2 packages Sloppy Joe seasoning mix (optional)
Salt, to taste
Toasted rolls or other crisp bread

In a heated, greased skillet, brown the meat. Put into a colander and drain off the grease. Put meat into slow-cooking pot with other ingredients, excepting bread over which dish will be served. Stir to mix well. Cover pot. Cook on low 8 to 10 hours, or on high 5 hours. If you think it is too liquidy, to thicken it remove the pot cover and set it on high for 30 minutes. Serve on toasted rolls or slices of any crisp bread.

BRISKET AND VEGETABLES

5 lbs. brisket
1 large onion, peeled, chopped
1 large carrot, peeled, chopped
2 tsp salt
1 bay leaf
1 cup water
½ tsp. thyme, whole
1 lb. small onions, peeled
6 medium carrots, peeled, cut into ½ inch strips

If brisket is too large to go into slow-cooking pot, cut it in half or roll it and tie with string. Add chopped onion, carrot, salt, bay leaf, thyme and water. Cover pot. Cook on low 10 to 12 hours. Test meat with fork, and when it is done remove it from pot. Keep meat warm. Into slow-cooking pot place the small onions and carrot strips. Cover pot. Cook on high 1 to 2 hours. With a slotted spoon, remove vegetables from pot, and place them around the meat on serving platter.

CHILI BEEF HASH

2 lbs. ground beef
2 medium onions, peeled, chopped
2 garlic cloves, peeled, minced
1 No. 2½ can tomatoes
1½ tsp chili powder
½ tsp salt
2 tsp Worcestershire sauce
1 cup raw rice
Cooked noodles or rice

In large, greased skillet brown the ground meat. Add onions, garlic and mushrooms, and sauté until onion is golden brown. Put in slow-cooking pot with remaining ingredients. Stir to mix well. Cover pot. Cook on low 6 to 8 hours, or on high 3 to 4 hours. Serve on cooked noodles or rice, which you have separately prepared.

BEEF STEW WITH CORN

2 lbs. stew meat, cut in cubes
1 tsp salt
¼ tsp pepper
½ tsp paprika
4 zucchini, sliced
2 cups hot water
2 Tbsp Worcestershire sauce
1 16-oz. can kernel corn, drained
3 Tbsp cornstarch
3 Tbsp water

Sprinkle salt, pepper and paprika over pieces of meat. Put meat in slow-cooking pot. Add zucchini. Pour hot water and Worcestershire sauce in pot. Cover pot. Cook on low 8 to 10 hours, or on high 4 to 5 hours. Put corn into pot and stir. In a cup mix cornstarch and water. Pour into pot. Cover pot. Cook on high 15 minutes.

STEAK WITH SOUR CREAM

2½ lbs. boneless round steak, cut
   in 2-inch pieces
Salt and pepper
1 beef bouillon cube, crushed
1 onion, peeled, sliced
½ cup water
¼ cup flour
¼ cup water
1 cup sour cream

Sprinkle salt and pepper over meat pieces. Place meat in slow-cooking pot. Add bouillon cube, onion and ½ cup water. Cover pot. Cook on low 6 to 8 hours, or on high 3 to 4 hours. Remove meat from pot. Dissolve flour in ¼ cup water. Put mixture in pot, and stir. Cover pot. Cook on high 10 minutes. Pour sour cream into pot, and stir. Turn off heat. When serving, pour sauce over meat.

BEEF WITH MACARONI ELBOWS

1½ lbs. ground beef
1 small onion, peeled, chopped
1 tsp salt
1 tsp Worcestershire sauce (optional)
¼ cup flour
1¼ cups hot water
2 tsp beef bouillon
2 Tbsp dry red wine
½ lb. cooked, elbow-shaped
   macaroni
1 2-oz. can sliced mushrooms,
   drained
1 cup sour cream

In skillet, on top of oven, brown meat and onion. Drain excess fat. Put meat and onion in slow-cooking pot. In a bowl mix salt, Worcestershire sauce and flour. Put mixture into pot, and stir. In a pitcher mix hot water, bouillon and wine. Pour into pot. Stir all in pot to mix well. Cover pot. Cook on low 2 to 3 hours. Put macaroni, mushrooms and sour cream into pot. Stir to mix well. Cover pot. Cook on high 15 minutes.

SWEDISH MEAT BALLS

1 lb. chuck, ground
¼ lb. pork, ground
¼ lb. veal, ground
   or ½ lb. of either, if only one
   other meat is desired in addition
   to beef.
1½ cups bread crumbs
1 cup milk or light cream
2 eggs
1 medium onion, peeled,
   chopped finely
1¾ tsp salt
¾ tsp dill weed
¼ tsp allspice
⅛ tsp nutmeg
3 Tbsp butter or margarine
 1 10½-oz. can beef broth
⅛ tsp pepper
½ cup light cream

Grind meats together. Soak bread crumbs in milk or cream 5 minutes. Mix together meats, eggs, onion, 1½ tsp salt, ¼ tsp dill weed, allspice and nutmeg. Refrigerate the mixture, covered, for 1 hour. Shape mixture into 1-inch balls, and in a skillet lightly brown them in heated butter. Place meatballs in slow-cooking pot. Add remaining ingredients, plus the pan drippings from the skillet. Cover pot. Cook on low 4 to 6 hours, or on high 1½ to 2½ hours.

Crock-Pot slow cooker courtesy of Rival Manufacturing Compa

POT AU FEU

3 medium onions, peeled
3 cloves
1½ cups parsley, peeled, chopped
1½ cups celery, sliced
1 garlic clove, peeled, chopped
2 8-oz. cans beef broth
2 lbs. beef, rump or pot roast, boneless
1 lb. pork tenderloin (or small pork chops)
2 chicken breasts or thighs, halved
Salt and pepper, to taste, and other seasonings as preferred

Stick a clove into each onion. Place in slow-cooking pot. Add parsnips, celery, garlic and beef broth. Trim off any excess fat on beef, pork and chicken. Place meats on top of vegetables. Add salt and pepper (or other seasonings) to taste. Cover pot. Cook on low 12 to 18 hours, or on high for 8 hours. Remove meat and vegetables from pot. Skim fat from liquid remaining in pot; this may be served as a soup, into which you may sprinkle chopped fresh parsley. Cut meats into serving pieces, before bringing to table. Serve meat with vegetables. If you prefer, you could separately prepare boiled potatoes, carrots, or whatever other favorite vegetables you enjoy, and place them on the serving platter with the meat. This is a flexible recipe, and you may delete some suggested ingredients and add others you prefer.

CHAPTER 5

LAMB AND VEAL RECIPES

IRISH STEW

3 lbs. stew meat, cut in 1½-inch
   cubes
4 cups water
2 tsp salt
¼ tsp pepper
5 medium potatoes, peeled, diced
10 carrots, peeled, sliced
2 small onions, peeled, sliced

Place all ingredients in slow-cooking pot. Stir to mix well. Cover pot. Cook on low 8 to
10 hours, or on high 4 to 5 hours. Before serving, stir food well. If you want to thicken the
sauce, in a cup of water mix 2 Tbsp flour or ¼ cup quick tapioca. Pour it into stew, stir well.
Cover pot. Cook about 15 minutes on high.

LAMB SHANKS

6 lamb shanks
2 Tbsp oil
1 tsp salt
½ tsp pepper
½ tsp garlic powder
Dash of paprika, rosemary,
marjoram (all optional)
Juice of ½ lemon
1 cup Sauterne wine
1 Tbsp cornstarch
¼ cup water

Ask butcher to cut shank bones in half. Trim off any excess fat on shanks, and in a large skillet with hot oil brown all sides of the shanks. Place meat in slow-cooking pot. Season meat with all listed seasonings, or any others you may prefer for taste. Add lemon juice and wine. Cover pot. Cook on low 10 to 12 hours, or on high 5 to 6 hours. About 15 minutes before serving, add cornstarch blended with water, to thicken gravy. Cover pot. Cook on high for these 15 minutes.

LEG OF LAMB

4 to 5 lbs. leg of lamb
2 10-oz. jars mint jelly
½ cup butter or margarine
4 Tbsp vinegar
2 tsp dry mustard

In a hot skillet, brown the lamb on all sides. In a saucepan melt mint jelly and butter, then stir in vinegar and mustard, and mix well. Place leg of lamb in slow-cooking pot, put the mint mixture over the leg on all sides. Cover pot. Cook on slow 8 to 9 hours, or on high 4 to 5 hours. Serve this dish with additional mint sauce or mint jelly.

BRAISED LAMB WITH NOODLES

2 lbs. boneless lamb shoulder,
    cut in cubes
2 garlic cloves, peeled, chopped
½ cup dry white wine
1½ tsp salt
⅛ tsp pepper
1 tsp oregano (optional)
2 medium onions, peeled,
    chopped
1 carrot, peeled, chopped
1 6-oz. can vegetable cocktail
    juice
Cooked noodles

In a skillet, on top of stove, brown the lamb pieces to remove excess fat. Remove lamb. Drain excess fat. Into same skillet put garlic and pour in wine. Stir while cooking to get brown bits left in skillet. Put lamb in slow-cooking pot. Sprinkle lamb with salt, pepper, oregano. Pour wine mixture into pot. Put onion and carrot in pot. Pour vegetable juice into pot. Stir all contents to mix. Cover pot. Cook on low 8 to 10 hours, or on high 4 to 5 hours. Serve on bed of noodles which you separately prepared.

LAMB STROGANOFF

2 lbs. lamb, cut in cubes
1 garlic clove, peeled, minced
½ cup onion, peeled, chopped
1 Tbsp paprika
1 tsp salt
½ tsp pepper
1 16-oz. can tomato sauce
1 tsp Worcestershire sauce
¼ tsp rosemary (optional)
1 cup sour cream
Cooked noodles or rice

Place all ingredients, excepting noodles and rice, in slow-cooking pot. Cover pot. Cook on low 6 to 8 hours, or on high 4 to 5 hours. (If you cook on low, it is all right to add the sour cream when placing the ingredients into the slow-cooking pot. But if you cook on high, then retain the sour cream and do not put it into pot until the last hour of cooking.) This dish is served on a bed of noodles or rice, which you have separately prepared.

VEAL STEW HAWAIIAN

3 lbs. veal, cut in 2-inch pieces
2 No. 2 cans pineapple cubes,
  drained
1 Tbsp seasoned salt
2 Tbsp paprika
2 bay leaves
½ tsp pepper
2 medium onions, peeled, sliced
2 cups water

Place all ingredients in slow-cooking pot. Stir to mix well. Cover pot. Cook on low 8 to 10 hours, or on high 4 to 5 hours. Before removing from pot to serve, stir well. If thicker sauce is desired, mix ¼ cup flour with 1 cup water, until creamy. Pour into stew, and stir. Cover pot. Cook on high approximately 15 minutes.

VEAL SCALLOPINI

2 lbs. boneless veal shoulder, cut
  into 1-inch cubes
½ cup flour
½ tsp salt
⅛ tsp pepper
¼ cup salad oil
1 cup onion, peeled, chopped
¾ cup mushrooms, whole,
  canned or fresh
1 No. 2½ can tomatoes
1 Tbsp fresh basil, chopped
1½ tsp salt
⅛ tsp pepper
½ tsp sugar
Cooked rice or spaghetti

Mix flour, ½ tsp salt and ⅛ tsp pepper, and coat the pieces of meat with mixture. Heat salad oil in skillet, and brown the coated meat pieces on all sides. Place meat in slow-cooking pot. Drain tomato cans and use juice to scrape the brown bits from the skillet. Add this and all other ingredients, excepting rice or spaghetti, to slow-cooking pot. Stir well to mix. Cover pot. Cook on low 8 to 9 hours, or on hot 4 hours. Serve over rice or spaghetti, which you have separately prepared.

LEG OF VEAL WITH WINE

2 Tbsp butter or margarine
1 garlic clove, peeled, minced
1 tsp salt
¼ tsp ground rosemary
Pinch of thyme
Pepper, to taste
5 lbs. leg of veal, boned and tied
2 onions, peeled, sliced fine
2 celery stalks, cut into 2-inch
  pieces
2 carrots, peeled, cut into 1-inch
  pieces
1 bay leaf
½ cup butter or margarine
1¾ cups water
¾ cup dry Sherry wine

Cream the 2 Tbsp butter with the seasonings. Rub this mixture into the meat. Place vegetables, bay leaf and 2 cups butter in slow-cooking pot. Over the vegetables place the leg of veal. Over the veal, pour water and wine. Cover pot. Cook on low 10 to 12 hours, or on high 5 to 6 hours. If you want to thicken gravy, mix 2 Tbsp flour with 1 cup of water, stir until creamy. About 15 minutes before cooking time is finished, pour this mixture into the meat juices, and stir. Cover pot. Cook on high for those 15 minutes.

POT ROAST

3 to 4 lbs. veal rump roast
1 Tbsp dry mustard
1 tsp poultry seasoning
1 Tbsp brown sugar
1 tsp salt
¼ tsp pepper
1 Tbsp flour
2 Tbsp salad oil
1 large onion, peeled, sliced
¼ cup water
1 bay leaf
3 Tbsp cider vinegar

Pat veal dry with towel. In a bowl mix the next six ingredients listed. Rub this mixture into the meat. In a skillet, heated with oil, brown the meat on all sides. Place meat in slow-cooking pot. On top of meat place onion slices. Into water put bay leaf and vinegar; pour this over the meat. Cover pot. Cook on low 6 to 8 hours, or on high 3 to 4 hours. Before serving, discard bay leaf. Slice meat thin and serve with any hot sauce you prefer.

CHINESE CASSEROLE

1 lb. veal, cubed
3 Tbsp flour
2 Tbsp oil
1½ cups celery, sliced
2 small onions, chopped
1 can cream of mushroom soup
1 can cream of chicken soup
1 cup water
2 Tbsp soy sauce
½ cup raw rice

Dredge veal pieces in flour. Heat oil in skillet, and brown veal in it. Place veal in slow-cooking pot with other ingredients. Cover pot. Cook on high for 1 hour; then on low for 6 to 8 hours.

Courtesy of Planters Peanut Oil

CHAPTER 6

PORK AND HAM RECIPES

PORK CHOP CASSEROLE

6 to 8 pork chops
Salt and pepper
2 medium white (or sweet)
  potatoes, peeled, sliced
1 large onion, peeled, sliced
1 large green pepper, seeded,
  sliced
½ tsp leaf oregano
¼ tsp whole thyme
1 1-lb. can tomatoes

Trim off excess fat on chops. Season with salt and pepper. In a heated skillet brown the chops on both sides. Drain chops on paper towel. Place chops in slow-cooking pot. In the order listed, add the other ingredients. Cover pot. Cook on low 8 to 10 hours, or on high 3 to 4 hours.

SAVORY ROAST

5 lbs. loin end pork roast
1 large onion, peeled, sliced
4 Tbsp sugar
¾ cup hot water
2 Tbsp soy sauce
2 Tbs. Sherry wine
½ tsp dried ginger
3 Tbsp wine vinegar
1 Tbsp ketchup
1 green pepper, seeded, chopped
Salt, pepper, garlic salt to taste
1 10½-oz. can pineapple chunks

Season roast with salt, pepper and garlic salt. Place roast into hot oven to broil for 20 minutes, to remove excess fat. Place onion in slow-cooking pot, on top of which place the roast and other ingredients, excepting pineapple. Cover pot. Cook on low 10 to 12 hours, or on high 4 to 5 hours. Add pineapple in last ½ hour of cooking.

PORK CHOPS WITH ORANGES

3 lbs. pork chops, lean
Salt and pepper to taste
3 oranges, sliced thin
1 cup fresh orange juice

Place chops in slow-cooking pot. Season chops with salt and pepper. Put orange slices on top of chops; pour in orange juice. Cover pot. Cook on low 6 to 8 hours, or on high 3 to 4 hours. When serving, use uncooked orange slices as a garnish.

PORK CHOPS WITH APPLES

2 1-lb. cans dry-pack sweet
  potatoes, sliced
2 1-lb. cans sliced apples
½ cup butter or margarine,
  melted
1 cup brown sugar
1 tsp ground ginger
8 loin pork chops
Salt and pepper to taste
1 cup water

Place sweet potatoes and apple in slow-cooking pot. Sprinkle with salt and pepper. Mix together butter, sugar and ginger; pour this mixture over sweet potatoes and apples. Place pork chops on top of this. Sprinkle salt and pepper over chops. Pour water into pot. Cover pot. Cook on low 8 to 10 hours, or on high 4 to 5 hours.

PORK CHOPS, CHICKEN FLAVORED

6 to 8 lean pork chops, 1-inch
   thick
½ cup flour
1 tsp salt
1½ tsp dry mustard
½ tsp garlic powder (optional)
2 Tbsp oil
1 can chicken and rice soup

Mix flour, salt, mustard and garlic powder. Dredge chops in this mixture. In a skillet with hot oil place the chops and brown them on both sides. Place chops in slow-cooking pot. Pour in soup. Cook on low for 6 to 8 hours, or on high 3 to 4 hours.

BARBECUED PORK CHOPS

6 to 8 thick, lean pork chops
⅔ cup water
½ cup ketchup
⅓ cup vinegar
1 tsp salt
1 tsp celery salt
½ tsp nutmeg
1 bay leaf

Place chops in slow-cooking pot. Combine all other ingredients in water, and pour over the chops. Cover pot. Cook on low 8 to 10 hours, or on high 4 to 5 hours.

PORK CHOPS WITH SAUCES

This is a simple recipe, where you choose one can of either of the following as a sauce for the pork chops: Either cream of mushroom soup, or sweet and sour sauce, or cream of chicken soup, or chicken-rice soup, or barbecue sauce. Brown both sides of the chops in a skillet with hot oil. Place the browned chops in slow-cooking pot. Over the chops pour any one of the forgoing sauces. Cover pot. Cook on low 6 to 8 hours, or on high 4 to 5 hours.

BARBECUED PORK ROAST

2 medium onions, peeled, sliced
4 to 5 lbs. pork roast
5 cloves
2 cups water
1 16-oz. bottle barbecue sauce
1 large onion, peeled, chopped

Trim off any excess fat on meat. Place all ingredients, excepting barbecue sauce and chopped onion, in slow-cooking pot. Cover pot. Cook on low 8 to 12 hours, or on high 4 to 6 hours. When meat is done, take from pot and remove fat and bone. Place meat back into slow-cooking pot. Add barbecue sauce and chopped onion. Cover pot. Cook on low 4 to 8 hours, or on high 3 hours. (It may be a good idea to do the first part of the cooking overnight, and the next day continue with the barbecue sauce and onions.)

PORK STEAK WITH VEGETABLES

6 pork steaks
1 Tbsp oil
1 can condensed cream of asparagus soup (undiluted)
½ cup chopped scallions
1 tsp salt
½ tsp pepper
⅓ cup water
6 medium potatoes, peeled, sliced
2½ cups shredded cabbage
½ cup light cream

In a skillet on top of stove heat the oil and brown the steaks on both sides. Drain off excess fat. In a bowl mix the soup, scallions, salt, pepper and water. Put a layer of pork in slow-cooking pot, then a layer of potatoes and cabbage, and alternate layers until all used up. Pour soup mixture into pot. Cover pot. Cook on low 4 to 6 hours, or on high 2 to 4 hours. Pour cream into pot. Cover pot. Cook on high 25 minutes.

PORK POT ROAST

4 to 5 lbs, loin of pork
Salt and pepper, to taste
1 garlic clove, peeled, sliced
2 medium onions, peeled, sliced
2 bay leaves
1 clove
1 cup hot water
2 Tbsp soy sauce (optional)

Rub salt and pepper into pork roast. With knife, make tiny slits in meat and insert slices of garlic. In your oven, place the meat in broiler pan for about 15 minutes to broil away excess fat. Place 1 sliced onion in bottom of slow-cooking pot. On top of onion put meat, then the rest of the onion and other ingredients. Cover pot. Cook on low 10 to 12 hours, or on high 5 to 6 hours. When done, remove the roast to a serving platter. If you want a thicker gravy, make a smooth paste of 2 Tbsp water and 2 Tbsp cornstarch. Put this mixture in slow-cooking pot. Cover pot. Cook on high approximately 15 minutes.

SWEET AND SOUR PORK

1½ lbs. pork steak, cut into strips
1 tsp paprika
1 Tbsp oil
3 Tbsp brown sugar
¼ cup powdered dry milk
2 Tbsp cornstarch
½ tsp salt
1 1-lb. can pineapple chunks,
   drained (save syrup)
⅓ cup vinegar
1 Tbsp soy sauce
1 Tbsp Worcestershire sauce
⅓ cup water
1 small onion, peeled, slice thin
1 green pepper, seeded, cut into
   strips
Cooked rice

Sprinkle paprika over pork strips, and brown meat in hot oil in skillet. Place meat in slow-cooking pot. In a bowl, mix together brown sugar, dry milk, cornstarch and salt. In a cup put the pineapple syrup, and if it doesn't measure to ⅔ of the cup add water to make it that amount. Then combine this syrup with the vinegar, soy sauce and Worcestershire sauce. Pour this liquid into the bowl of mixed dry ingredients, and stir to mix. Add this to the pork in slow-cooking pot, then the onion, and stir all. Cover pot. Cook on low 6 to 8 hours, or on high 4 hours. About 1½ hours before serving, add pineapple chunks and green pepper strips. Serve the pot roast over cooked rice, which you will have separately prepared.

CHINESE PORK STEAK

1½ lbs. pork steak, cut into strips
2 Tbsp oil
1 large onion, peeled, sliced
1 small green pepper, seeded, cut
   into strips
1 4-oz. can mushrooms, drained
1 8-oz. can tomato sauce
3 Tbsp brown sugar
1½ Tbsp vinegar
1½ tsp salt
2 tsp Worcestershire sauce
Cooked rice

In heated oil in a skillet place pork strips, toss them around to brown and remove excess fat. Drain strips on towel. Place meat and remaining ingredients, except rice, in slow-cooking pot. Cover pot. Cook on low 6 to 8 hours, or on high 4 hours. Serve over cooked rice, which you have separately prepared.

SPARERIBS AND SAUERKRAUT

3 to 4 lbs. lean pork spareribs,
   cut in serving pieces
Salt and pepper, to taste
1 10½-oz. can sauerkraut
½ small head of cabbage, sliced
   thin
1 large onion, peeled, sliced thin
1 large apple, quartered, cored,
   sliced
1 tsp dill weed or caraway seeds
1 cup water
½ tsp salt

Sprinkle salt and pepper on spareribs. Place spareribs in broiler pan in your oven, or in a skillet, to brown them to remove excess fat. Put a layer of spareribs at bottom of slow-cooking pot, then a layer of sauerkraut, cabbage, onion and apple. Repeat layers with spareribs, and the other ingredients over it. Add dill weed or caraway seeds to water, then pour this over all in pot. Cover pot. Cook on low 6 to 8 hours, or on high 4 to 5 hours. If you cook on high, during cooking stir the food a few times. (If you do not want to combine both sauerkraut and cabbage, this could be made with either one.)

Courtesy of Planters Peanut Oil

CHINESE SPARERIBS

4 lbs. spareribs
⅓ cup soy sauce
2 Tbsp ketchup
⅓ cup orange marmalade
1 garlic clove, peeled, crushed

In a bowl mix soy sauce, ketchup, marmalade and garlic. Brush sauce on both sides of meat. Put meat in slow-cooking pot. Pour into pot remaining sauce. Cover pot. Cook on low 8 to 10 hours, or on high 4 to 5 hours.

44

BARBECUED SPARERIBS

3 lbs. spareribs, cut in serving
   pieces
¼ tsp salt
¼ tsp pepper
1 large onion, peeled, sliced
1 clove garlic, peeled, minced
2 cups or cans barbecue sauce

Place spareribs in broiler pan in your oven, or in a skillet, to brown the meat and remove excess fat. Sprinkle spareribs with salt and pepper. Place ribs in slow-cooking pot. Add onion, garlic and barbecue sauce. Cover pot. Cook on low 6 to 8 hours, or on high 3 to 4 hours.

SAVORY HAM STEAK

2 slices ham, ¾ inch thick
1 cup sweet cider
1 cup port wine (optional)
½ cup maple syrup
¾ cup cranberries
¾ cup grapes or raisins, seedless
4 cloves
Juice of 1 orange
Slices of canned pineapple

Place ham slices in slow-cooking pot. Add all ingredients, except pineapple. Cover pot. Cook on high for 1 hour, then on low for 6 hours. If you want to thicken gravy, remove ham to serving platter. Mix 3 Tbsp water and 2 Tbsp cornstarch and form a paste. Stir this into liquid in slow-cooking pot, and cook approximately 15 minutes on high until desired thickness is achieved. When serving ham, add pineapple slices as garnish and for extra good taste.

HAM AND POTATO SCALLOP

6 ham slices, ¼ inch thick
6 to 8 medium potatoes, peeled,
   sliced thin
1 cup onion, peeled, chopped
Salt and pepper to taste
1 cup grated American or other
   similar processed cheese
1 10½-oz. can cream of celery
   soup, undiluted
Paprika, to taste

Place half the ham, potatoes and onions in slow-cooking pot. Sprinkle with salt and pepper. Then sprinkle with half the grated cheese. Repeat layers. On top of this spread the soup. Sprinkle with paprika. Cover pot. Cook on low 8 hours, or on high 4 hours.

HAM-STUFFED PEPPERS

6 small green peppers, tops cut
   off, seeded
1 lb. ground ham
⅓ cup raw rice
⅔ cup water
½ cup onions, chopped
½ tsp salt
¼ cup ketchup
1 cup water
4 carrots, peeled, cut in 3-inch
   pieces
Cooked rice

Sprinkle salt in cavities of peppers. In a bowl mix together the ham, rice, water, onion, salt and ¼ ketchup. Stuff this mixture into peppers, about ⅔ full. Place the peppers in slow-cooking pot; you may have to put them on top of one another. Place the carrot sticks in pot, using them to prop up the peppers. Pour into pot the 1 cup ketchup and ½ cup water. Cover pot. Cook on low 6 to 8 hours, or on high 3 hours. Serve the peppers on a bed of cooked rice, which you have separately prepared. Over this pour the sauce left in pot.

HAM WITH WINE

4 lbs. fresh whole ham
1 garlic clove, peeled, sliced
Salt and pepper, to taste
¾ Tbsp caraway seeds
3 medium onions, peeled, sliced
2 carrots, peeled, sliced
2 celery stalks, sliced
1 bay leaf
2 cloves
¾ cup water.
¾ dry white wine

With knife, score the ham, in a diamond pattern. Rub ham on all sides with garlic, salt, pepper and caraway seeds. Place vegetables, bay leaf and clove on bottom of slow-cooking pot. Place ham on top of vegetables. Pour water and wine over ham. Cover pot. Cook on low 10 to 12 hours, or on high 6 to 8 hours.

KNOCKWURST AND CABBAGE

6 knockwursts, cut in 2-inch
  pieces
1 small head cabbage, shredded
1 onion, peeled, sliced thin
1 tsp caraway seeds (optional)
½ tsp salt
2 cups chicken bouillon

Put layer of meat pieces in slow-cooking pot. On top of meat put layer of cabbage and onions. Alternate layers of meat and vegetables. Sprinkle with salt and caraway seeds. Pour bouillon into pot. Cover pot. Cook on low 5 to 6 hours, or on high 2½ to 3 hours.

HAM AND CORN CASSEROLE

¼ cup butter or margarine
¼ green pepper, seeded, chopped
¼ cup flour
½ tsp paprika
¾ tsp salt
¼ tsp pepper
⅛ tsp ground thyme
⅛ tsp marjoram
½ tsp dry mustard
2 cups milk
1 8-oz. can cream-style corn
2 cups cooked potatoes, diced
1 medium onion, peeled,
  chopped
2 cups cooked ham, diced
1 cup American cheese (or other
  similar processed cheese),
  grated

On top of your stove, in a saucepan melt butter; add green pepper and sauté. Stir in flour and seasonings. Slowly stir in milk and cook until thick. Place the mixture, with remaining ingredients, in slow-cooking pot. Stir well. Cover pot. Cook on low 6 to 8 hours, or on high 3 to 4 hours.

Courtesy of Planters Peanut Oil

49

SMOKED HAM IN FOIL

This is a basic recipe for cooking ham, which may then be served in whatever way you prefer. Start with a precooked whole ham, sprinkle it with liquid smoke, then wrap it in aluminum foil. Place ham in slow-cooking pot. Cook on low for 6 to 12 hours. (You may omit the liquid smoke if you want ham plain.)

HAM WITH PINEAPPLE

2 lbs. slice of ham, center cut, 1-
   inch thick
Cloves
1 tsp dry mustard
1 2-lb. can pineapple chunks
½ cup brown sugar
1 cup red wine wine

Push cloves into ham, spaced 2 inches apart. Place ham in slow-cooking pot. On top of ham put mustard, pineapple, brown sugar. Pour wine over all. Cover pot. Cook on low 6 to 8 hours. Before serving, remove cloves from ham.

SAUSAGE AND HAM STEW

½ lb. sausage meat
½ lb. cooked ham, cut in cubes
 2 15-oz. cans black-eye peas (do
   not drain)
1 onion, peeled, minced
2 Tbsp minced parsley
¼ cup dry white wine

In a skillet, on top of oven, place the pork to brown. Drain excess fat. Put a layer of sausage in slow-cooking pot. Over it a layer of all other ingredients, and repeat this in alternate layers of sausage and the others. Pour wine over all in pot. Cover pot. Cook on low 5 to 7 hours, or on high 2½ to 3½ hours. Serve in soup bowls.

CHAPTER 7

POULTRY RECIPES

While these are mainly recipes built around chicken, they may also be used for turkey or other fowl, and you could adapt some of your favorite recipes for the slow-cooking pot.

ROAST CHICKEN

6½ lbs. roasting chicken
Salt and pepper, to taste
Parsley, chopped
¼ cup butter or margarine, melted
Basil (optional)

Wash the chicken, and pat dry with a towel. Sprinkle the inside of the bird with salt, pepper and parsley. Fold legs and wings across breast of chicken, tie them with string. Place breast side up in slow-cooking pot. Brush skin of chicken with melted butter. Sprinkle parsley (and basil, if included) on chicken. Cover pot. Cook on high for 1 hour; then on low 8 to 10 hours. (You can save the broth to be used in soup or gravy.)

CHICKEN AND MUSHROOMS

6 medium chicken breasts
Salt, pepper, paprika, to taste
½ cup Vermouth or dry white
 wine (optional)
1 10½-oz. can condensed cream
 of mushroom soup, undiluted
1 4-oz. can slice mushrooms,
 drained
1 cup sour cream
¼ cup flour
Cooked rice or noodles

Lightly sprinkle chicken breasts with salt, pepper and paprika. Place chicken in slow-cooking pot. Thoroughly mix wine, soup and mushrooms. Separately mix sour cream and flour; then stir in the sour cream mixture only if you are going to cook on low. (If you will cook on high, withhold the cream, and add it to the pot 30 minutes before the cooking will be finished.) Pour the mixture over the chicken. Sprinkle with paprika. Cover pot. Cook on low 6 to 8 hours, or on high 3 to 4 hours. Serve chicken and its sauce on cooked rice or noodles, which you have separately prepared.

CHICKEN WITH WINE

2½ lbs. broiler chicken, cut up
1 tsp salt
¼ tsp pepper
½ tsp dried marjoram (optional)
1½ Tbsp chopped shallots (optional)
1 garlic clove, peeled, crushed
6 small medium onions, peeled
¼ lb. mushrooms, halved
2 cups white wine
½ cup chicken broth
1 Tbsp tomato paste
1 Tbsp parsley, chopped (optional)
6 new potatoes, peeled

In a skillet, heated with oil seasoned with salt, pepper and shallots, brown the chicken pieces. Place onions, mushrooms and garlic in bottom of slow-cooking pot. Add chicken with shallots, marjoram, wine and broth. Cover pot. Cook on low 6 to 8 hours, or on high 3 to 4 hours. Sprinkle parsley on chicken, before serving.

ROAST CHICKEN WITH CARROTS

1 6-oz. pkg prepared dressing
Water
¼ cup sauterne (or similar) white
   wine
10 medium carrots, peeled, in 2-
   inch slices
1 5-lb. roasting chicken
Salt and pepper to taste

In a saucepan on the stove prepare dressing with water as directed on the package. Let it cool, then pour wine into saucepan, and stir to mix. Dry chicken and stuff it with dressing. Put carrots in slow-cooking pot. Place chicken on top of carrots. Sprinkle with salt and pepper. Cover pot. Cook on low 6 to 8 hours, or on high 3 to 4 hours.

CHICKEN WITH ZUCCHINI

1 fryer chicken, cut in parts
¼ cup flour
½ tsp salt
⅛ tsp pepper
½ tsp paprika
2 Tbsp grated processed cheese
1 lb. zucchini, sliced thin
½ cup chicken bouillon
1 4-oz. can mushrooms, drained

Sprinkle salt on chicken parts. In a bowl mix flour, salt, pepper, paprika and cheese. Coat chicken with mixture. Put zucchini in slow-cooking pot. Pour bouillon into pot. Put in chicken parts, spread over zucchini. Cover pot. Cook on low 5 to 6 hours, or on high 2½ to 3 hours. Put mushrooms in pot. Cover pot. Cook on high 15 minutes.

CHICKEN AND HAM STEW

1 3-lb. chicken, cut in parts
2 qts water
2 cups cooked ham, cut in cubes
1 onion, peeled, chopped
3 potatoes, peeled, diced
1 10-oz. pkge frozen lima beans,
  partially thawed
1 10-oz. pkge frozen kernel corn,
  partially thawed
2 tsp salt
¼ tsp pepper
1 tsp sugar

Put chicken in slow-cooking pot. Add water, ham, onion and potatoes. Stir all to mix. Cover pot. Cook on low 4 to 5 hours, or on high 2 to 2½ hours. Remove chicken pieces from pot. Cut or pick the chicken meat from the bones. Put chicken into pot, and discard the bones. Add all other ingredients to pot. Cover pot. Cook on high 1 hour.

CHICKEN PARMIGIANA

6 halves chicken breasts
1 egg, beaten
1 tsp .salt
¼ tsp pepper
1 cup bread crumbs
1 medium eggplant, in ¾-inch
  slices
1 10½-oz. can pizza sauce
6 slices mozzarella cheese
Grated Parmesan or other
  processed cheese

In a bowl beat salt and pepper with egg. Dip each half-breast chicken in mixture, then dip into bread crumbs to form a coating. In a skillet, on top of stove, sauté chicken and butter. Put eggplant in slow-cooking pot, then place chicken on top of eggplant. Pour pizza sáuce into pot. Cover pot. Cook on low 6 to 8 hours, or on high 3 to 4 hours. Put mozzarella cheese in pot. Sprinkle grated cheese on top. Cover pot. Cook on high 10 to 15 minutes.

56

CHICKEN CACCIATORE

2 medium onions, peeled, slice thin
2½ to 3 lbs. broiler fryer chicken, cut up
2 garlic cloves, peeled, minced
1 1-lb. can tomatoes
1 8-oz. can tomato sauce
1 tsp salt
¼ tsp pepper
1½ tsp crushed oregano
½ tsp crushed basil
1 bay leaf
¼ cup dry white wine
Cooked spaghetti, butter sauce

Place onions in slow-cooking pot. On top of onions place chicken pieces, garlic, tomatoes, tomato sauce, salt, pepper, herbs and wine. Cover pot. Cook on low 6 to 8 hours, or high 3 to 4 hours. Serve chicken with its sauce on spaghetti, which you have separately prepared.

CHICKEN WITH ORANGE SAUCE

5 lbs. chicken parts
Salt, pepper, paprika, to taste
2 8-oz. cans whole onions,
    drained
1 cup carrots, peeled, cut in 2-
    inch pieces
1 cup celery, chopped
2 3-oz. cans sliced mushrooms,
    drained
2 Tbsp brown sugar
½ tsp ground ginger
1 6-oz. can frozen orange juice
    concentrate, thawed

On chicken parts sprinkle salt, pepper and paprika. Place chicken and vegetables in slow-cooking pot. Thoroughly mix sugar, ginger and orange juice, and pour over chicken. Cover pot. Cook on high 45 minutes; then on low 6 to 8 hours.

TURKEY ROLL WITH CRANBERRIES

2 Tbsp cornstarch
¼ cup sugar
1 cup fresh cranberries, ground
¾ cup orange marmalade
2½ lb. frozen turkey roll, partially thawed
Salt and pepper

On top of stove, in a saucepan, mix cornstarch and sugar, then add cranberries and marmalade. Stir until mixture thickens and bubbles. Put turkey in slow-cooking pot. Sprinkle turkey with salt and pepper. Pour the hot sauce over turkey. Cover pot. Cook on low 8 to 10 hours, or on high 4 to 5 hours. Before serving, slice turkey. Serve with sauce.

TURKEY TETRAZZINI

3 cups cooked turkey, diced
1 small onion, peeled, chopped
  fine
¼ cup white wine
2 cups chicken or turkey broth
1 10-oz. can cream of mushroom
  soup
¾ cup almonds, slivered,
  blanched
1 8-oz. can mushrooms, drained
1 cup pitted ripe olives, sliced
Parmesan or American cheese,
  grated
Cooked spaghetti or macaroni

Place all ingredients, excepting cheese, olives and spaghetti, in slow-cooking pot. Cover pot. Cook on high 1 hour, then on low for 6 to 8 hours. Add olives at the last half hour of cooking. Place cooked spaghetti or macaroni in a greased baking dish. Put turkey and sauce over it, sprinkle with grated cheese. Place under broiler in oven until it is lightly browned.

ROAST DUCKLING, BURGUNDY

5 lbs. duckling, whole or cut in
   parts
¼ Burgundy wine
1 Tbsp melted butter or
   margarine
1 Tbsp Worcestershire sauce
¼ cup lemon juice
1 tsp salt
¼ tsp pepper
1 clove garlic, peeled, minced
   (optional)
1 tsp marjoram, crushed (optional)

Prick skin of duckling with a fork over all the surface. Put a metal trivet or rack in bottom of slow-cooking pot. On top of that, put the duckling with skin side up. In a bowl combine remaining ingredients, mix well. Brush skin of duckling with half of the sauce. Cover pot. Cook on low 7 to 9 hours, or on high 3½ to 4½ hours. (If possible, half way through the cooking, uncover pot to remove excess fat and to add more sauce to the skin of the duckling, also to turn the duckling.) About 30 minutes before end of cooking time on low, or 15 minutes if cooking on high, brush the duckling with the remaining sauce. Cover pot. Finish cooking.

60

CHICKEN IN POT

1 3 lb. chicken (whole or cut up,
    as you prefer)
2 carrots, peeled, sliced
2 onions, peeled, sliced
2 celery stalks with leaves, cut
    in 1-inch pieces
2 tsp salt
½ tsp pepper
½ cup chicken broth, or water, or
    white wine
½ tsp basil (optional)

Place carrots, onions and celery in slow-cooking pot. Add chicken. Over it sprinkle salt and pepper, then pour liquid on it. Over it sprinkle basil. Cover pot. Cook on low 7 to 8 hours, or on high 2½ to 3½ hours. (Save leftover broth for soup base.)

CHICKEN CURRY

3 to 4 chicken breasts, halved
Poultry seasoning, to taste
Paprika, to taste
1 chicken boullion cube
1 cup boiling water
¼ cup Sauterne or other dry
   white wine
1 tsp onion, minced
½ tsp curry powder
Pepper, to taste
1 3-oz. can sliced mushrooms,
   drained

Place chicken breasts in slow-cooking pot. Sprinkle them with poultry seasoning and paprika. Dissolve boullion cube in water; add to it the wine, seasonings and mushrooms. Pour liquid mixture over chicken. Cover pot. Cook on high for 45 minutes; then on low 6 to 8 hours.

CHICKEN HASH

2 cups cooked chicken, chopped
2 small onions, peeled, chopped
2 small potatoes, peeled,
   chopped
2 carrots, peeled, chopped
2 eggs
1 tsp salt
3 Tbsp parsley, chopped
¾ tsp poultry seasoning, or sage
1½ cups chicken gravy

In the food grinder chop finely the chicken, onion, potato and carrots. Add remaining ingredients, and thoroughly mix. Place all in slow-cooking pot. Cover pot. Cook on low 8 to 10 hours, or on high 4 to 5 hours.

CHICKEN ESPAÑOL

3 to 4 lbs. chicken, cut up
Salt, pepper, paprika, to taste
Garlic salt, to taste (optional)
1 6-oz. can tomato paste
½ can beer
1 small jar pimiento-stuffed
  olives, with liquid
Cooked rice or noodles

Sprinkle chicken parts with salt, pepper and paprika. Place chicken in slow-cooking pot. Mix tomato paste and beer; then pour over chicken. Add olives and liquid to pot. Cover pot. Cook on low 7 to 9 hours, or high 3½ to 4½ hours. Serve on rice or noodles, which you have separately separately prepared.

STUFFED CORNISH HEN

6 Cornish hens (if frozen, thaw
  hens)
1 8-oz. pkge stuffing mix
¾ cup melted butter or
  margarine
2 Tbsp brown sugar
2 Tbsp soy sauce
2 Tbsp lime juice
2 Tbsp dry white wine

Make stuffing according to directions on package. Fill each hen with stuffing. In a bowl mix the remaining ingredients. Brush this mixture over skin of the hens, leaving some of the sauce for later brushing. Put metal rack or trivet in bottom of slow-cooking pot. Place hens on rack. Cover pot. Cook on low 5 to 7 hours, or on high 2½ to 3½ hours. (If possible, part-way through cooking, uncover pot and brush hens with remaining sauce.)

BARBECUED TURKEY DRUMSTICKS

6 drumsticks (raw)
Salt and pepper
1 Tbsp minced onion
¼ cup ketchup
2 Tbsp Worcestershire sauce
¼ cup vinegar
¼ cup molasses

Sprinkle salt and pepper on drumsticks. Put drumsticks in slow-cooking pot. In a bowl mix all other ingredients. Pour mixture over turkey. Cook on low 5 to 7 hours, or on high 2½ to 3½ hours. When serving turkey, pour sauce over the drumsticks.

CHICKEN WITH HAM

3 to 4 lbs. chicken, cut up
Salt, pepper, paprika, to taste
1 large onion, peeled, chopped
1 small green pepper, seeded, chopped
2 small garlic cloves, peeled, minced
1 small can pimiento, diced
½ tsp chili powder
2 chicken bouillon cubes
1 cup diced ham (or ½ lb. precooked pork sausages)
1 cup raw rice
1 10-oz. pkge frozen peas, thawed

Sprinkle salt, pepper and paprika over chicken parts, as seasoning. Place chicken and all ingredients, excepting rice and peas, in slow-cooking pot. Cover pot. Cook on low 6 to 10 hours, or on high 4 hours. About 1½ hours before serving, add rice and peas. Cover pot. Cook on high until rice is tender.

65

MEXICAN CHICKEN

10 to 12 tortillas, cut into 6
    pieces
4 cups chopped cooked chicken
1 can condensed cream of
    mushroom soup, undiluted
½ green pepper, cut into strips
1 Tbsp minced onion
1 cup sour cream
1¼ cups grated processed cheese
Shortening (to grease inside of
    pot)

Use shortening to thinly grease the bottom and sides of slow-cooking pot. In a bowl mix all ingredients except tortillas and grated cheese. Place tortillas on bottom of slow-cooking pot. On top of layer of tortillas put a layer of the mixture of the other ingredients then alternate layers of tortillas and the mixture. Sprinkle grated cheese over all in pot. Cover pot. Cook on low 4 to 5 hours, or on high 2 to 2½ hours.

CHICKEN LOAF

2½ to 3 lbs. raw chicken, ground
2 eggs
1 tsp. horseradish
¼ cup evaporated milk

In a bowl combine all ingredients, mix well, then form a round loaf about 6 inches in diameter. Put the loaf in slow-cooking pot. Cover pot. Cook on low 5 to 6 hours, or on high 2½ to 3 hours.

JAMBALAYA (CHICKEN AND SHRIMP)

1 broiler-fryer chicken, cut in
    parts
1 12-oz. can tomatoes, mashed
1 carrot, peeled, sliced
1 clove garlic, peeled, minced
1 tsp salt
⅛ tsp pepper
½ tsp oregano (optional)
½ tsp basil (optional)
1 lb. shrimp, raw, shelled
2 cups cooked rice

Put chicken and all other ingredients (excepting shrimp and rice) in slow-cooking pot. Cover pot. Cook on low 4 to 5 hours, or on high 2 to 2½ hours. Place shrimp and rice in slow-cooking pot. Cover pot. Cook on high 35 minutes.

CHAPTER 8

SEAFOOD RECIPES

FISH IN SOUR CREAM

1½ lbs. halibut or swordfish
    steak (or 1 lb. package frozen
    fillets, thawed)
Salt and pepper, to taste
2 Tbsp oil
1 cup cooked string beans (or 1
    No. 2 can white potatoes,
    drained)
¼ cup onion, peeled, minced
3 medium tomatoes, peeled,
    sliced
1 cup sour cream
½ tsp dry mustard
1 Tbsp lemon juice
¼ tsp salt
⅛ tsp pepper
Dash of paprika

Sprinkle salt and pepper on fish. On bottom of slow-cooking pot spread 1 Tbsp oil before you place the fish, then spread the fish with the remaining oil. Place vegetables in pot. In a bowl mix the sour cream with the mustard, lemon juice, salt and pepper. Pour this mixture over the vegetables in pot. Sprinkle with paprika. Cover pot. Cook on high 1 hour, then on low 4 to 6 hours.

SEAFOOD COMBINATION IN WINE

1 can condensed mushroom soup
1 cup water
1 cup dry white wine
2 tsp instant onion flakes
1 tsp dill weed
¼ tsp paprika
¼ tsp Tabasco sauce
⅔ cup canned shrimp, drained
½ cup canned pimiento, drained,
    diced
1½ cups canned tuna
1 cup canned crabmeat, drained,
    cartilege removed
1½ cups raw instant rice
¼ cup parsley, chopped

In a bowl combine the soup, wine, water and seasonings. Place the fish and other ingredients, excepting parsley, in slow-cooking pot. Pour liquid over all. Cover pot. Cook on low 2 to 3 hours. Garnish with parsley.

SHRIMP MARINARA (WITH SPAGHETTI)

1 16-oz. can peeled tomatoes,
    mashed
1 6-oz. can tomato paste
1 clove garlic, peeled, minced
1 tsp salt
¼ tsp pepper
½ tsp oregano
1 lb. cooked shrimp, shelled
Cooked spaghetti
Grated processed cheese

Put all ingredients (excepting shrimp, spaghetti and cheese) in slow-cooking pot. Stir to mix well. Cover pot. Cook on low 6 to 7 hours, or on high 3 to 3½ hours. Put shrimp in pot, stir to mix. Cover pot. Cook on high 15 minutes. Serve over bed of spaghetti, sprinkle with grated cheese.

Courtesy of Planters Peanut Oil

SHRIMP CASSEROLE

¼ lb. fresh mushrooms, sliced
2 Tbsp butter or margarine
2 5-oz. canned shrimp, rinsed, deveined (or 1 lb. cooked fresh shrimp, shelled, deveined)
1½ cups cooked rice
1½ cups grated American processed cheese (or other similar cheese)
½ cup evaporated milk, undiluted
3 Tbsp ketchup
½ tsp Worcestershire sauce
¼ tsp salt
⅛ tsp pepper

On top of stove, in a skillet, sauté mushrooms in butter until tender, (approximately 10 minutes). Combine mushrooms with other ingredients, and lightly mix. Place all in slow-cooking pot. Cover top. Cook on low 2 to 3 hours, or on high 1 to 1½ hours.

69

SPICY SHRIMP

1½ to 2 lbs. fresh shrimp, in
   shells (or frozen shrimp,
   thawed)
3 cups water (or beer)
1 Tbsp salt
1½ Tbsp mixed pickling spices
   (or 1 packet shrimp spices)

You have a choice of two ways of cooking this recipe. The first one is to place all ingredients in slow-cooking pot. Cover pot. Cook on low 3 to 5 hours. Or else, place into slow-cooking pot the water (or beer), salt and spices. Cover pot. Cook on low all day (or all night). Then add shrimp, and cook on high 30 to 45 minutes (or until shrimp turn pink in color).

SHRIMP CREOLE

½ garlic clove, peeled, minced
2 green peppers, seeded,
   chopped
2 small onions, peeled, chopped
2 Tbsp oil
1 8-oz. can tomato sauce
¼ tsp paprika
¼ tsp chili powder
½ tsp Worcestershire sauce
½ Tbsp salt
¼ tsp pepper
1 bay leaf
1 Tbsp parsley, chopped
1 No. 2 can tomatoes, drained,
   chopped
1 cup cooked (or canned) shrimp,
   shelled, deveined
Cooked rice

In a skillet, with heated oil, brown the garlic, green peppers and onions. Place these in slow-cooking pot. Into the tomato sauce mix paprika, chili powder, Worcestershire sauce, salt, pepper, bay leaf and parsley. Pour into pot, then place tomatoes in pot. Cover pot. Cook on low 6 to 8 hours. An hour before finish of cooking time, place shrimp in pot. Cover pot. Cook to time of serving. This dish is served over cooked rice, which you have separately prepared.

CURRIED SHRIMP AND CRABMEAT

1 12-oz. can crabmeat, drained,
    cartilege removed, flaked
1 12-oz. can medium shrimp,
    drained
1 8-oz. can water chestnuts,
    drained, sliced
⅓ cup light cream
¼ cup Sherry wine
1 egg, beaten
1 10-oz. frozen shrimp soup,
    thawed
2 scallions with tops, chopped
    fine
Salt and pepper, to taste
Toast points or cooked rice

Place crabmeat and shrimp in slow-cooking pot. Add other ingredients, excepting toast or rice, and slightly stir to mix. Cover pot. Cook on high 1 hour; then on low 4 to 6 hours. Serve on toast points, or on cooked rice, which you have separately prepared.

CRABMEAT IN WINE

1 12-oz. can crabmeat, drained,
    cartilege removed, flaked (or
    same amount of frozen crab-
    meat, thawed)
3 Tbsp butter or margarine
¼ cup dry Sherry wine
¼ cup light cream
1 egg, beaten
1 can cream of mushroom soup
½ tsp Worcestershire sauce
2 scallions with tops, chopped
    fine
Salt and pepper, to taste
Toast points or patty shells

Place crabmeat in slow-cooking pot. Add other ingredients, excepting toast points or patty shells. Lightly stir to mix. Cover pot. Cook on high 1 hour; then on low 4 to 6 hours. Serve on toast points or in patty shells, which you have separately prepared. (The patty shells may be purchased ready-made.)

LOBSTER A LA NEWBURG

1 can condensed cream of shrimp soup
¾ cup evaporated milk (undiluted), or light cream
2 egg yolks, beaten
1 5-oz. can lobster, flaked (or frozen lobster, thawed)
1 4-oz. can sliced mushrooms, drained
2 Tbsp Sherry wine
Cooked rice, or chow mein noodles, or pastry shells

Place all ingredients, excepting cooked rice, chow mein noodles and pastry shells, in slow-cooking pot. Mix thoroughly. Cover pot. Cook on low 4 to 6 hours. Serve over rice, or noodles, or in pastry shells, which you have separately prepared. (The noodles and pastry shells may be purchased ready to use.)

SHRIMP A LA NEWBURG

Follow the ingredients and method of cooking as told in the preceding recipe for Lobster a la Newburg; but instead of the lobster, substitute 1½ cups of cooked shrimp, drained and deveined.

73

BOUILLABAISSE (FRENCH FISH STEW)

½ cup olive oil (or oil of your preference)
2 tsp salt
1 Tbsp paprika
Pinch of dried basil
1 Tbsp garlic, peeled, chopped
½ cup onion, peeled, chopped
½ cup celery, chopped
1 1-lb. can tomatoes
1 8-oz. can tomato sauce
2 cups water
½ cup dry Sherry or white wine
1½ lbs. medium shrimp (leave shell on)
3 halibut or sea bass steaks, cut in 1-inch pieces
1 lb. crabmeat
4 medium lobster tails (leave shell on)
1 lb. clams (leave shell on) or scallops (optional)

Place all ingredients, excepting the seafood, in slow-cooking pot. Cover the pot. Cook on high 2 to 4 hours. Then add seafood. Cover pot. Cook on high 3 to 4 hours. (You may prefer to substitute other seafood, instead of some of those listed here; if so, choose fish which are generally of their same type and texture.)

SALMON AND CHEESE CASSEROLE

1 lb. can salmon, with liquid
1 4-oz. can mushrooms, drained
1½ cups bread crumbs
2 eggs, beaten
1 cup grated American cheese
1 Tbsp lemon juice
1 Tbsp onion, minced
1 Tbsp butter or margarine, melted

In a bowl flake the salmon, remove bones. Add all ingredients excepting the butter, to the bowl and thoroughly mix. With butter grease the bottom of the inside of the slow-cooking pot. Place the salmon mixture in pot. Cover pot. Cook on low 3 or 4 hours, or on high 1½ to 2 hours.

TUNA AND NOODLE CASSEROLE

1 8-oz. pkg noodles (cooked to tender, drained)
2 cans condensed cream of celery or cream of mushroom soup
½ cup dry Sherry wine, or milk
¼ cup milk
1 pkg frozen mixed vegetables, thawed
1 Tbsp parsley, minced
2 7-oz. cans tuna, drained
½ cup almonds, toasted, sliced (optional)
1 Tbsp butter or margarine, melted

In a bowl thoroughly mix soup, wine or milk, additional ¼ cup milk, vegetables, parsley, tuna. Into this mixture fold the cooked noodles. With butter grease the bottom of the inside of the slow-cooking pot. Place the tuna mixture in pot. Sprinkle almonds on top. Cover pot. Cook on low 6 to 8 hours, or on high 3 to 4 hours.

OYSTER STEW

1 qt milk
¼ cup butter or margarine
2 tsp salt
½ tsp Worcestershire sauce
2 Tbsp flour mixed with 2 Tbsp water (optional)
1 pt shelled oysters, with liquid
Cayenne pepper, to taste (optional)

Place all ingredients in slow-cooking pot, excepting the oysters. (If you want a thick stew, include the mixture of flour and water; but this could be omitted.) Cover pot. Cook on high 1½ hours. Remove cover. Thoroughly stir contents in pot. Place oysters in pot. Cover pot. Cook on low 2 to 4 hours. Sprinkle cayenne pepper over each individual serving dish, if desired.

PAELLA (SPANISH FISH AND CHICKEN)

Before you start this recipe, have ready a cooked chicken (it is suggested you cook it according to Chicken In Pot recipe given in Chapter 7). After it is cooked remove it from the broth; remove the bones, and cut chicken meat into pieces. Proceed with the paella:

1 3-lb. cooked chicken, boned,
   cut in pieces
2 cups water
1 cup raw rice
2 garlic cloves, peeled, crushed
½ cup butter or margarine or oil
¼ cup pimiento, cut in strips
½ tsp oregano
½ tsp saffron
¾ lb. raw frozen shrimp, shelled
   (do not thaw)
1 8-oz. can shelled clams, or tuna

In a skillet on top of your stove, heat butter or oil, and in it fry the rice and garlic until rice is browned. Place this, with all other ingredients, in slow-cooking pot. Thoroughly stir, to mix well. Cover pot. Cook on low for 6 to 8 hours, or on high 2 to 3 hours.

Courtesy of The Pan American Coffee Bureau

CHAPTER 9

SOUP AND CHOWDER RECIPES

BEAN SOUP

1 lb. dry navy beans (soaked
  overnight in water to cover,
  drained)
2 qts water
1 lb. meaty ham bone, or pieces
  of ham
Salt, to taste
1 cup onion, chopped
1 bay leaf (optional)
½ cup celery leaves, chopped
Pepper, to taste (or 5 peppercorns)

Place all ingredients in slow-cooking pot. Cover pot. Cook on low 10 to 12 hours, or on high 5 to 6 hours. Remove ham bone, trim the meat off it, and return the pieces of meat into the soup. Remove from soup, before serving, the bay leaf, peppercorns and celery sprigs. (This makes 8 to 10 servings.)

SPLIT PEA SOUP

Use preceding recipe given for Bean Soup, but substitute 1 lb. green split peas (soaked overnight in water and drained) in place of beans.

VEGETABLE AND MEAT SOUP

1 to 2 lbs. beef shanks, oxtails,
    short ribs or veal bones
1 1-lb. can tomatoes
2 carrots, peeled, sliced
3 stalks celery, with tops, sliced
2 medium onions, peeled, diced
2 medium potatoes, peeled, diced
3 cups water
1 tsp salt
4 peppercorns (or pepper, to
    taste)
3 beef bouillon cubes
1 10-oz. frozen mixed vegetables
    or lima beans or peas (op-
    tional).

Place all ingredients, excepting frozen vegetables, in slow-cooking pot. Stir to mix well.
Cover pot. Cook on low 8 to 10 hours, or on high 4 to 6 hours. If you include frozen vegetables,
add them to the pot during the last 2 hours (if cooking on slow) or the last hour (if on high).

CHICKEN AND VEGETABLE SOUP

2 lbs. chicken wings and backs
    (or other parts)
2 qts hot water
1 Tbsp salt
½ tsp pepper
3 carrots, peeled, quartered
3 stalks celery, sliced
1 medium onion, peeled,
    chopped fine

Place all ingredients in slow-cooking pot. Cover pot. Cook on low 6 to 8 hours, or on high 3 to 4 hours. Before serving, remove meat from chicken bones. Return meat to soup. Discard bones.

MACARONI AND GROUND BEEF SOUP

1 lb. ground beef, separated in
    chunks
1 tsp salt
¼ tsp pepper
¼ tsp basil (optional)
¼tsp oregano (optional)
1 envelope onion soup mix (un-
    diluted)
3 cups boiling water
1 9-oz. can tomato sauce
1 cup celery, sliced
1 cup carrots, peeled, sliced
1 cup cooked macaroni
¼ cup grated processed cheese

Put beef in slow-cooking pot. Add salt, pepper, basil, oregano and soup mix to pot. In a bowl mix water, tomato sauce and soy sauce. Pour mixture into pot. Add celery and carrots to pot. Cover pot. Cook on low 6 to 8 hours, or on high 3 to 4 hours. Put macaroni and cheese in pot. Cover pot. Cook on high 15 minutes.

BAKED BEAN SOUP

1 12-oz. can baked beans
1 16-oz. can stewed tomatoes
6 strips bacon, cooked, chopped
2 Tbsp bacon drippings
2 Tbsp chopped onion
1 tsp salt
1 Tbsp vinegar
1 Tbsp brown sugar

Put all ingredients in slow-cooking pot. Stir to mix well. Cover pot. Cook on low 4 to 6 hours, or on high 2 to 3 hours.

LENTIL AND VEGETABLE SOUP

2 cups dry lentils (soaked over-
    night in water, drained)
5 cups water
2 bacon slices, diced
1 medium onion, peeled,
    chopped
1 carrot, peeled, sliced thin
2 stalks celery, with tops, sliced
1 garlic clove, peeled, minced
2 tsp salt
¼ tsp pepper
½ tsp oregano, crushed
1 1-lb. can tomatoes

Place all ingredients in slow-cooking pot. Stir to mix well. Cover pot. Cook on low 8 to 10 hours, or on high 4 to 6 hours. Adjust seasoning before serving.

MINESTRONE SOUP

½ cup onion, minced
1 garlic clove, peeled, minced
2 Tbsp parsley, minced
1 cup ham, minced
½ cup salt pork, diced fine
1 qt water
1 qt chicken broth
1 medium tomato, peeled, seed-
    ed, diced
½ cup celery, diced
½ cup carrots, peeled, diced
1 medium potato, peeled, diced
1 cup spinach, diced
½ cup cooked chick peas or navy
    beans
¼ cup uncooked elbow macaroni
¼ cup grated Parmesan cheese
    (or other cheese you prefer)

Place all ingredients, excepting macaroni and cheese, in slow-cooking pot. Cover pot. Cook on low 6 to 8 hours, or on high 4 to 5 hours. Half an hour before serving, add macaroni and cheese to pot. Before serving, adjust seasoning to taste.

81

ONION SOUP

1 qt beef bouillon
3 cups onions, sliced thin
¼ cup butter or margarine
1 tsp salt
¼ cup sugar
2 Tbsp flour
¼ cup dry Vermouth or cognac
  (optional)
Slices of thinly cut French
  bread, toasted (optional)
1 cup grated Parmesan cheese
  (or other cheese of your
  choice)

Melt butter in skillet, add onion slices. Cover skillet, let onions cook. Add to skillet the salt, sugar, flour and Vermouth. Stir to mix well. Place bouillon in slow-cooking pot. Add the onion mixture to pot. (Reserve the toast and cheese.) Cover pot. Cook on low 6 to 8 hours, or on high 3 to 4 hours. When serving, add on top of each soup dish a toast slice and sprinkling of cheese.

POTATO SOUP

6 medium potatoes, peeled, cut
  in large cubes
2 leeks, washed, cut into large
  cubes
2 medium onions, peeled,
  chopped
1 carrot, peeled, sliced
1 stalk celery, sliced
4 chick bouillon cubes
1 Tbsp parsley flakes
5 cups water
1 Tbsp salt
Pepper, to taste
⅓ cup butter or margarine
1 13-oz. can evaporated milk
Chives, chopped

Place all ingredients, excepting milk and chives, in slow-cooking pot. Cover pot. Cook on low 10 to 12 hours, or on high 4 to 5 hours. During last hour of cooking stir in evaporated milk. When serving, sprinkle top of soup dish with chives. (If you prefer, remove potato chunks from soup before serving, mash the potatoes, then add to soup and stir well.)

GROUND BEEF SOUP

2 Tbsp butter or margarine
1 lb. beef, coarsely ground
2 Tbsp butter or margarine
2 cups water
2 small onions, peeled, chopped
3 stalks celery, chopped
2 carrots, peeled, diced
1 1-lb. can tomatoes
½ tsp pepper
1 10-oz. frozen mixed vegetables, thawed
½ cup butter or margarine, melted
½ cup flour

In a skillet melt butter and brown the beef in it, then drain off fat. Place the meat and all other ingredients, excepting the ½ cup melted butter and flour, in slow-cooking pot. Cover pot. Cook on low 8 to 10 hours. One hour before serving, set pot on high. Mix together the melted butter and flour to make a smooth paste. Stir mixture into pot. Cook 15 minutes on high.

BEAN AND POTATO SOUP

1 cup dried beans (red preferred)
6 cups water
3 potatoes, peeled, diced
2 onions, peeled, sliced
1 clove garlic, peeled, minced
1 8-oz. can tomato paste
3 beef bouillon cubes
¼ lb. salt pork, sliced
1 tsp salt
¼ tsp allspice (optional)

Soak beans in water overnight. Put beans and water in slow-cooking pot. Cover pot. Cook on low 4 to 6 hours, or on high 2 to 3 hours. Put all other ingredients in pot. Cover pot. Cook on low 6 to 8 hours, or on high 4 to 6 hours.

BEEF, VEGETABLE AND NOODLE SOUP

½ lb. stew meat, cut in cubes
1 8-oz. can tomato sauce
1 16-oz. can stewed tomatoes
1 pkge onion soup mix
1 cup water
1 10-oz. pkge frozen mixed
    vegetables, partially
    thawed
½ cup uncooked 1-inch pieces
    of noodles

Put meat, tomato sauce, stewed tomatoes, soup mix and water in slow-cooking pot. Cover pot. Cook on low 6 to 8 hours, or on high 3 to 4 hours. Put in pot frozen vegetables and noodle pieces. Cover pot. Cook on high 30 minutes.

CHICKEN NOODLE SOUP

Chicken carcass, broken into
    parts
1 carrot, peeled, chopped
1 onion, peeled, chopped
2 celery stalks, chopped
2 qts water
1 tsp salt
½ tsp marjoram
1 Tbsp dried parsley
    tied in a cheesecloth bag
1 bay leaf
1 cup cooked noodles

Put all ingredients (excepting noodles) in slow-cooking pot. Cover pot. Cook on low 5 to 6 hours, or on high 2½ to 3 hours. Take spice bag and carcass out of pot. Scrape off any meat on bones, and put these meat pieces into pot. Put noodles into pot. Cover pot. Cook on high 20 minutes. (This soup can also be made with a turkey carcass.)

LAMB AND CABBAGE SOUP

1 lamb shank
1 beef bouillon cube
½ cup carrots, peeled, diced
½ cup celery, sliced
1 large potato, peeled, diced
½ cup scallions, chopped
½ tsp salt
¼ tsp pepper
4 cups water
4 cups shredded cabbage

Put all ingredients (excepting cabbage) in slow-cooking pot. Stir to mix well. Cook on low 6 to 8 hours, or on high 3 to 4 hours. Take meat from pot. Scrape meat off bone, and return meat to pot. Discard bone. Skim fat from top of soup. Put cabbage in pot. Cover pot. Cook on high 20 to 25 minutes. (Other meat, instead of the lamb, can also be used to make this soup.)

Courtesy of McIlhenny Company   Tabasco

CHICKEN DUMPLING SOUP

2 lbs. chicken wings and backs
  (or other parts)
6 cups hot water
1 stalk celery, chopped
2 carrots, peeled, shredded
1 Tbsp salt
½ tsp pepper
1 medium onion, peeled,
  chopped fine
1 cup packaged biscuit mix
1 Tbsp minced parsley
6 Tbsp milk

Put chicken, water, celery, carrots, onion, salt and pepper in slow-cooking pot. Stir to mix well. Cover pot. Cook on low 5 to 7 hours, or on high 2½ to 3½ hours. Remove chicken parts from pot. Scrape off meat, return meat to pot, discard bones. In a bowl mix the biscuit mix, parsley and milk until the contents is blended and moist. With a teaspoon drop the dumpling mixture into slow-cooking pot. Cover pot. Cook on high 30 minutes.

CREAM OF CAULIFLOWER SOUP

1 medium cauliflower, cut into
  flowerets
1 onion, peeled, chopped
1 stalk celery, in 1-inch slices
4 cups chicken broth
1 tsp salt
⅛ tsp pepper
1 cup light cream

Put all ingredients (excepting cream) in slow-cooking pot. Cover pot. Cook on low 6 to 8 hours, on high 3 to 4 hours. Puree contents in a blender; or crush through a sieve to obtain a thick liquid. Return puree to pot. Pour cream into pot. Cover pot. Cook on high 10 minutes.

CHEESE SOUP WITH BEER

2 cups chicken broth
¼ cup green pepper, chopped
¼ cup onion, peeled, chopped
¼ cup carrot, peeled, chopped
¼ cup celery, chopped
2 Tbsp butter or margarine
1 tsp salt
¼ tsp pepper
⅓ cup flour
2 Tbsp water
3 cups grated sharp cheddar or
  other processed cheese
1 can beer (not iced)

Put all ingredients (excepting flour, water, cheese and beer) in slow-cooking pot. Cover pot. Cook on low 5 to 6 hours, or on high 2½ to 3 hours. Strain the soup, returning the liquid to the pot and putting the vegetables in a blender to puree them (or crush through a sieve to obtain a thick liquid). Return the puree to slow-cooking pot. In a bowl mix flour and water, then add this paste to pot. Put cheese in pot, stirring slowly to mix well with contents in pot. Pour beer into pot. Cover pot. Cook on high 20 minutes.

PEANUT SOUP

4 cups chicken bouillon
1 medium onion, chopped
⅓ cup celery, chopped
⅓ cup peanut butter
2 Tbsp butter or margarine
¼ tsp salt
1 cup light cream or milk
⅓ cup flour
⅓ cup water
Chopped peanuts, unsalted (op-
    tional)

Put bouillon, onion, celery, peanut butter, butter and salt in slow-cooking pot. Cover pot. Cook on low 4 to 6 hours, or on high 2 to 3 hours. In a bowl mix cream, flour and water. Add this mixture to pot. Stir to mix well. Cover pot. Cook on high 15 minutes. (Remove cover and stir to make a smooth thickness, two or three times through this 15 minutes.) Sprinkle chopped peanuts over soup, when serving (if desired).

BEEF AND LENTIL SOUP

1½ lbs. beef shank
1 cup dry lentils (soaked over-
    night in water, drained)
4 cups water
4 beef bouillon cubes, crushed
2 tomatoes, peeled, chopped
1 onion, peeled, chopped
3 carrots, peeled, chopped
2 celery stalks, chopped
2 medium potatoes, peeled,
    cubed
1 tsp salt
¼ tsp pepper
2 small zucchini, chopped
½ cabbage head, shredded

Put all ingredients (excepting zucchini and cabbage) in slow-cooking pot. Stir to mix well. Cover pot. Cook on low 8 to 10 hours, or on high 4 to 5 hours. Take meat from pot. Scrape meat off bone, return meat to pot, discard bone. Put zucchini and cabbage in pot. Cover pot. Cook on high 35 minutes.

BASIC BEEF SOUP

1½ lbs. beef shank
8 cups water
1 carrot, peeled, chopped
1 onion, peeled chopped
½ cup chopped celery
2 Tbsp chopped parsley
¼ tsp thyme
4 peppercorns
1 bay leaf
1 garlic clove, peeled, quartered

Put all ingredients in slow-cooking pot. Cover pot. Cook on low 6 to 8 hours or on high 3 to 4 hours. Take meat from pot. Scrape meat off from bone, return meat to soup, discard bone. Remove cheesecloth bag from pot and discard.

BEEF AND KIDNEY BEAN SOUP

6 cups basic beef soup (see preceding recipe)
2 16-oz. cans kidney beans, drained
1 green pepper, cored, seeded, sliced

Put all ingredients in slow-cooking pot. Cover pot. Cook on high 1 hour.

CHEESE SOUP

2 cans cream soup (mushroom, chicken or celery)
1 cup milk (or beer)
1 lb. American processed cheese, cubed (or other cheese you prefer)
1 tsp Worcestershire sauce
¼ tsp paprika
Toasted croutons

Place all ingredients, excepting croutons, in slow-cooking pot. Cover pot. Cook on low for 4 to 6 hours, or on high 2 to 3 hours. When serving, top each soup dish with croutons.

MANHATTAN CLAM CHOWDER

¼ lb. salt pork or bacon, diced
1 large onion, peeled, chopped
2 medium potatoes, peeled, diced
2 carrots, peeled, sliced thin
3 stalks celery, sliced
1 Tbsp parsley flakes
1 12-oz. can tomatoes
1 1-lb. can (or 2 cups fresh, shelled) clams, with liquid
2 peppercorns (or pepper to taste)
1 bay leaf
1 tsp dry thyme, crushed

In skillet on top of oven, fry pork or bacon to remove excess fat; then drain. Place all ingredients in slow-cooking pot. Cover pot. Cook on low 8 to 10 hours, or on high 4 to 5 hours.

SEAFOOD CHOWDER

¼ lb. salt pork or bacon, diced
2 lbs. fresh or frozen (thawed) cod or haddock or other fish fillets
4 medium potatoes, peeled, cubed
1 medium onion, peeled, chopped
1 tsp salt
¼ tsp pepper
1 13-oz. can evaporated milk

In a skillet on top of oven fry the pork or bacon, to remove excess fat, then drain. Place all ingredients, excepting evaporated milk, in slow-cooking pot. Cover pot. Cook on low 6 to 8 hours, or on high 3 to 4 hours. Add milk to pot during last hour of cooking.

NEW ENGLAND (or BOSTON) CLAM CHOWDER

Follow the preceding recipe for Seafood Chowder; but instead of the 2 lbs. of fish substitute 1 1-lb. can (or 2 cups fresh, shelled) clams with their liquid.

ASPARAGUS AND LEEK CHOWDER

½ cup water
3 Tbsp flour
1   10-oz. pkge frozen cut
    asparagus, thawed
3 large leeks, sliced
3 cups mushrooms, sliced
3 cups chicken broth
4 Tbsp butter or margarine
½ tsp salt
¼ tsp pepper
1 12-oz. can white corn (whole
    kernel)
1 Tbsp pimiento, minced
2 cups milk
1 cup light cream

Mix flour and water to a paste. Place in slow-cooking pot with all other ingredients, excepting cream. Cover pot. Cook on low 6 to 8 hours, or on high 3 to 4 hours. Just before serving, add cream to pot and stir well.

Courtesy of Planter's Peanut Oil

BOUILLABAISSE

This dish is often classed with the Chowder recipes. But some prefer to think of it as a main dish. Recipe is given in Chapter 7.

PUREED VEGETABLE CHOWDER

1 10-oz. pkge frozen peas, thawed
2 medium potatoes, peeled, cubed
6 leeks, sliced
3 cups bouillon (chicken or beef)
2 Tbsp butter or margarine
1 tsp salt
¼ tsp pepper
¾ cup sour cream

Put all ingredients (excepting sour cream) in slow-cooking pot. Cover pot. Cook on low 6 to 8 hours, or on high 3 to 4 hours. Slowly pour chowder into a blender to make a puree. Or slowly form a puree by putting mixture through a sieve. Pour puree back into pot. Pour in cream, and stir to mix well. Cover pot. Cook on high 15 minutes.

CORN CHOWDER

2 16-oz. cans kernel corn, drained
2 potatoes, peeled, diced
1 onion, peeled, chopped
2 cups chick bouillon
1 tsp salt
¼ tsp pepper
2 cups milk
¼ cup butter or margarine

Put all ingredients (excepting milk and butter) in slow-cooking pot. Cover pot. Cook on low 6 to 8 hours, or on high 3 to 4 hours. Put milk and butter in pot. Stir to mix well. Cover pot. Cook on high 1 hour.

CHAPTER 10

VEGETABLE RECIPES

To cook in the slow-cooking pot, prepare fresh vegetables by washing or peeling and cutting them up or quartering them, as you do in the conventional way of cooking. Or you may use frozen vegetables, thawed. The simple method to use, unless a recipe gives other specific directions, is to place vegetables in the slow-cooking pot, then adding ½ cup of water (excepting 2 cups of water for artichokes). Cover pot. Cook on high 45 minutes; then on low 2 to 4 hours. It is good to occasionally stir the vegetables in the pot. If time does not permit you to do that, you may wrap the vegetables in foil before you place them in slow-cooking pot. the sides of the pot, then add the meat.

NEW BOILED POTATOES

3 lbs. new potatoes
4 cups water
1 tsp salt

Do not peel potatoes. Wash the skins thoroughly, to remove any rough spots as well as dirt on the skins. Place all ingredients in slow-cooking pot. Cover pot. Cook on high 3 hours, or on slow 6 hours. (If you use more or less potatoes, adjust the amount of water so it comes almost to the top of potatoes.)

BAKED POTATOES

6 large baking potatoes
Melted butter or margarine

Do not peel potatoes. Thoroughly scrub the skins to remove any rough spots and dirt. Grease the skins with the butter. Place potatoes in slow-cooking pot. Do not add water. Cook on low 8 to 10 hours; unless you have to speed up the time, then cook on high 4 to 5 hours.

STUFFED BAKED POTATOES

6 baked potatoes (use preceding
   recipe)
½ cup sour cream
3 Tbsp butter, softened
½ cup milk
1 tsp salt
⅛ tsp pepper
2 Tbsp grated processed cheese
Chives, chopped

Cut a wide slice, lengthwise, off top of each baked potato. Scoop out the insides of the potatoes, putting the pulp into a bowl. Add other ingredients (excepting cheese and chives). Stir contents of bowl until smoothness is produced. With a spoon fill each potato shell with the mixture. Sprinkle tops of potatoes with cheese. Set potatoes in a baking pan, and bake in the oven at 425°, for 15 minutes, until tops are lightly browned. (You may omit this oven browning, if you desire). When serving, top potatoes with chives.

HOT POTATO SALAD

6 large potatoes, peeled, sliced
1 large onion, peeled, sliced
1 tsp salt
Water
5 slices bacon, diced
2 Tbsp flour
2 Tbsp sugar
1 tsp dry mustard
½ tsp salt
¼ tsp pepper
¼ cup vinegar
⅔ cup water
½ tsp celery seeds (optional)

Put potato and onion slices in slow-cooking pot. Sprinkle salt on top. Pour water into pot to cover vegetables. Cover pot. Cook on low 5 to 6 hours, or on high 2½ to 3 hours. Remove food from pot, draining off liquid. Put food into a bowl. In a skillet on top of the stove, cook bacon pieces. Add to the skillet the flour, sugar, mustard, salt and pepper. Stir well. Add to skillet vinegar, water and celery seeds (if included). Stir well. Pour the mixture over potatoes in bowl, and thoroughly mix.

BAKED SWEET POTATOES

Do not peel potatoes. Thoroughly scrub the skins to remove any rough spots and dirt. Place potatoes in slow-cooking pot. Add ¼ cup water. Cover pot. Cook on high 1 hour; then on low 6 to 8 hours. Test potatoes for tenderness, as it may be necessary to cook longer if they are not done enough.

ACORN SQUASH

Wash the skin of the squash. Place squash whole in slow-cooking pot. Add ¼ cup water. (Or you may split the squash in half, then wrap in foil, before placing into pot.) Cover pot. Cook on high 1 hour; then on low 6 to 8 hours. When done, split the squash in half, remove seeds. Then sprinkle the inside of squash with salt, also cinnamon if you desire, and put in a dab of water.

POTATO AND CHEESE CASSEROLE

2 lbs. hashed brown potatoes (which you prepared in advance), or a 2-lbs. pkge frozen hashed brown potatoes, partly thawed
2 10-oz. cans cheese soup
1 13-oz. can evaporated milk, undiluted
1 can French fried onion rings
Salt and pepper, to taste
2 Tbsp butter or margarine

Grease bottom of slow-cooking pot with butter. In a bowl, mix together potatoes, soup, milk and ½ can onion rings. Place the mixture in slow-cooking pot. Sprinkle with salt and pepper. Cover pot. Cook on low 8 to 9 hours, or on high 4 hours. When serving, crumble the remaining ½ can onion rings, and sprinkle on top of the food.

SPINACH AND CHEESE CASSEROLE

2 10-oz. pkges frozen spinach,
   thawed, drained
2 cups cottage cheese, cream
   style
½ cup butter or margarine, cut
   into small pieces
1½ cups American processed
   cheese, cubed
3 eggs, beaten
¼ cup flour
1 tsp salt

In a bowl mix well all ingredients. Grease the slow-cooking pot with butter. Place ingredients in pot. Cover pot. Cook on high 1 hour, then on low 4 to 6 hours.

CARROTS AND CHEESE

2 lbs. carrots, peeled, ½ inch
   slices
1 medium onion, peeled, sliced
1 tsp salt
⅔ cup water
1 Tbsp flour
½ cup additional water
4 Tbsp butter or margarine
1 cup grated American process
   cheese (or Cheddar)
½ cup bread crumbs, buttered

Place carrots, onions, salt and ¼ cup water in slow-cooking pot. Cover pot. Cook on low 8 to 10 hours, or high 4 to 5 hours. One hour before serving, mix water and flour to thick paste, then pour the mixture into the pot over the vegetales. Thoroughly stir to mix all in pot. Add to pot the cheese and dots of butter. Cover pot. Cook on high about 15 minutes (until cheese melts). Stir contents in pot to mix well. Sprinkle top of food with bread crumbs. Cover pot. Cook on low additional 30 minutes.

Courtesy of Planter's Peanut Oil

MUSHROOM CASSEROLE

1 lb. mushrooms, medium size
1 Tbsp marjoram, chopped (optional)
1 tsp chives, minced
1 tsp salt
$\frac{1}{8}$ tsp pepper
$\frac{1}{2}$ cup butter or margarine, melted
$\frac{1}{2}$ cup chicken bouillon
$\frac{1}{4}$ cup dry white wine

Wash mushrooms. Place them in slow-cooking pot. Mix melted butter with marjoram, chives, salt and pepper. Place mixture in pot. Add bouillon and wine. Stir all to mix well. Cover pot. Cook on low 2½ to 3 hours, or on high 1 hour.

RED CABBAGE AND APPLES

1 small head red cabbage, washed, sliced coarsely
1 medium onion, peeled, chopped
3 apples (tart), peeled, cored, quartered
2 tsp salt
1 cup hot water
1½ Tbsp sugar
½ cup vinegar
3 Tbsp butter or margarine (or bacon grease)

Place all ingredients, in the order listed, in slow-cooking pot. Cover pot. Cook on low 8 to 10 hours, or high 3 hours. Before serving, thoroughly stir ingredients in pot.

SWEET & SOUR RED CABBAGE

4 slices bacon, diced
2 Tbsp flour
¼ cup brown sugar
1 tsp salt
⅛ tsp pepper
1 cup vinegar
½ cup water
1 medium red cabbage, shredded
1 onion, peeled, chopped

In a skillet on top of stove, brown the bacon pieces. Remove bacon, and set it aside. Put into the slow-cooking pot 1 Tbsp bacon drippings from the skillet, and add flour, sugar, salt and pepper. Stir to mix well. Pour vinegar and water into pot. Stir. Add cabbage and onion to pot. Cover pot. Cook on low 3 to 4 hours, or on high 1½ to 2 hours. Sprinkle bacon pieces on top of food when serving.

SAUERKRAUT AND BACON

4 slices bacon, diced
1 No. 2 (29 oz.) can sauerkraut
1 medium cabbage, chopped
1 onion, peeled, chopped
1 Tbsp butter or margarine
½ tsp salt
⅛ tsp pepper
1 tsp sugar

In a skillet on top of stove, brown the bacon. Do not drain off excess fat. Put in slow-cooking pot all ingredients (excepting bacon). Pour bacon pieces and drippings into pot. Cover pot. Cook on low for 3 to 5 hours, or on high ½ to 2½ hours.

STRING BEAN CASSEROLE

2 lbs. string beans, washed, cut into 1-inch pieces
1 can cream of mushroom soup, undiluted
1 can French fried onion rings
1 cup grated American process cheese
1 can water chestnuts, sliced thin
Slivered almonds (optional)
½ cup water

Place ingredients in slow-cooking pot in layers, in the order they are listed, and make three layers. (Reserve some of the onion rings.) Add water. Cover pot. Cook on low 10 to 14 hours, or on high 4 to 5 hours. About 15 minutes before serving, crumble the remaining onion rings and sprinkle them over food in pot. Cover pot. Continue cooking to done. (You may substitute 4 packages of cut-up frozen green beans instead of the fresh. In that case, thaw the beans before placing in slow-cooking pot, and cook on low 8 to 10 hours or on high 4 to 5 hours.)

BAKED CORN PUDDING

1 16-oz. can whole kernel corn,
  drained
3 eggs. lightly beaten
2 cups hot milk
1 Tbsp butter or margarine,
  melted
1 Tbsp minced onion
1 tsp sugar
1 tsp salt

In a bowl, mix all ingredients. With butter, grease inside of a 1½ qt baking pan. Cover the pan with a metal lid to fit, or with aluminum foil tied down to stay in place. Put a metal rack or trivet in bottom of slow-cooking pan. Put baking pan on top of rack. Pour 4 cups hot water around the baking pan in pot. Cover pot. Cook on low 4 to 5 hours, or on high for 2 to 2½ hours.

STRING BEANS WITH HAM

2 lbs. string beans, washed, cut
  in 1-inch pieces
3 cups water
1 tsp salt
¼ lb. bacon pieces (or ham, diced)

Place all ingredients in slow-cooking pot. Stir to mix well. Cover pot. Cook on low 10 to 12 hours, or on high 2 to 4 hours.

MASHED TURNIPS AND POTATOES

4 turnips, peeled, quartered
4 potatoes, peeled, quartered
1 tsp salt
1 Tbsp minced onion
Water
2 Tbsp butter or margarine, softened
1/4 cup light cream
1/2 tsp salt
1/8 tsp pepper

Put turnips, potatoes, salt and onion in slow-cooking pot. Pour in water to cover the vegetables. Cover pot. Cook on low 6 to 8 hours, or on high 3 to 4 hours. Drain vegetables and put into bowl. Add to bowl butter, cream, salt and pepper. Mash vegetables and beat mixture to fluffy smoothness.

STEWED TOMATOES

12 medium tomatoes, peeled, cut in quarters
3/4 Tbsp onions, chopped
1 tsp salt
1/2 tsp paprika
2 tsp brown sugar
1 tsp basil
2 Tbsp butter or margarine
3 slices white bread, crusts cut off, broken into small pieces

Place all ingredients, excepting bread pieces, in slow-cooking pot. Stir to mix well. Cook on low 6 to 8 hours, or on high 3 to 4 hours. During the last hour of cooking, place bread pieces in pot (to thicken the stew) and stir all ingredients. Cover pot. Continue cooking.

STRING BEANS WITH TOMATOES

¼ lb. salt pork, diced
2 lbs. string beans, broken into 3
  pieces
2 medium tomatoes, peeled,
  seeded, cubed
2 cups beef bouillon
½ tsp sugar
¼ tsp pepper

Put pork pieces in slow-cooking pot. Spread the pieces to cover bottom of top. Put tomato cubes on top of pork. Add remaining ingredients. Cover pot. Cook on low 6 to 8 hours, or on high 3 to 4 hours. Before serving, drain off the liquid.

SUMMER SQUASH AND TOMATOES

10 summer squash, sliced thin
⅓ cup sliced scallions
½ green pepper, cored, chopped
2 medium tomatoes, peeled,
  chopped
1 cup chicken bouillon
3 slices cooked crisp bacon,
  crumbled
¼ cup bread crumbs

Sprinkle salt over squash. Put into slow-cooking pot alternate layers of squash, scallions, peppers and tomatoes. Pour bouillon into pot. Put bacon and bread crumbs on top. Cover pot. Cook on low 4 to 6 hours, or on high 2 to 3 hours.

ARTICHOKES

6 artichokes
Salt, to taste (¼ tsp salt for each
   artichoke)
2 Tbsp vinegar or lemon juice
2 cups hot water

Wash artichokes, cut off the tips of leaves, also cut off about 1-inch from top. Place artichokes (standing upright) in slow-cooking pot. Add salt. Pour in water and vinegar (or lemon juice). Cover pot. Cook on low 8 to 10 hours, or on high 2 to 4 hours. Serve with melted butter and lemon juice, or whatever sauce you prefer, into which the heart and the torn-off leaves of the artichokes are dipped.

EGGPLANT CASSEROLE

1 large onion, peeled, sliced
1 garlic clove, peeled, minced
1 small or medium eggplant,
   peeled, cut in ½ inch cubes
3 medium zucchini, sliced thin
1 green pepper, seeded, sliced
1 12-oz. can peeled tomatoes,
   drained, cut in quarters (reserve juice)
Salt, to taste
1 Tbsp basil (optional)
2 Tbsp parsley flakes
2 Tbsp olive oil (or other oil you
   prefer)

Place a portion of all vegetables in slow-cooking pot, to form the first layer. Sprinkle on top a portion of the salt, basil and parsley. Repeat by layering the vegetables, then sprinkle with seasonings. When all layers in pot, pour over them juice from can of tomatoes. Over all the food, drizzle the oil. Cover pot. Cook on low 6 to 8 hours, or on high 3 to 4 hours.

SUMMER SQUASH AU GRATIN

2 lbs. summer squash, in ¼-inch
  slices
Water
1 tsp salt
¼ cup butter or margarine
2 cups croutons
½ cup grated processed cheese

Put squash in slow-cooking pot. Add water to cover squash. Add salt. Cover pot. Cook on low 3 to 4 hours, or on high 1½ to 2 hours. Remove squash, drain off liquid. In a skillet on top of stove, melt the butter. Add croutons to skillet, and stir to mix until croutons are browned. Add cheese to skillet Sprinkle the crouton-cheese mixture over the squash when serving.

SUMMER SQUASH AND ZUCCHINI

1½ lbs. summer squash, in ½-
  inch slices
1½ lbs. zucchini, in ½-inch slices
½ tsp salt
¼ tsp pepper
¼ cup butter or margarine
3 Tbsp bread crumbs
3 Tbsp grated processed cheese

Put zucchini and squash in slow-cooking pot. Sprinkle with salt and pepper. Put dabs of butter on top of squash. Sprinkle with crumbs and cheese. Cover pot. Cook on low 6 to 8 hours, or on high 3 to 4 hours.

VEGETABLE STEW

2 10-oz. pkges frozen mixed
  vegetables, partially thawed
½ cup celery, chopped fine
2 cans condensed cream of celery soup
1 small onion, peeled, chopped
1 beef or chicken bouillon cube
2 Tbsp butter or margarine,
  melted
½ cup water

Put mixed vegetables and celery in slow-cooking pot. In a bowl mix all other ingredients, then pour mixture into pot. Cover pot. Cook on low 4 to 5 hours, or on high 2 to 2½ hours.

PARSNIPS, ORANGE FLAVORED

6 large parsnips, peeled, cut in
  thin sticks
1 tsp salt
Water
2 Tbsp butter or margarine
⅓ cup orange juice
a Tbsp honey

Put parsnip sticks and salt in slow-cooking pot. Pour water into pot to cover parsnips. Cover pot. Cook on low 4 to 6 hours, or on high 2 to 3 hours. Drain water, remove parsnips to serving platter. In a saucepan, on top of stove, melt the butter, add orange juice and honey. Stir well, bring to a boil. Pour the mixture over parsnips before serving.

CARROTS, ORANGE FLAVORED

Following the preceding recipe for parsnips, orange flavored, substitute 6 large carrots, peeled and sliced thin.

CORN AND CHILI TAMALES

1 16-oz. can kernel corn, drained
1 16-oz. creamed corn
1 4-oz. can chopped green chilis,
  drained
1 onion, peeled, chopped
4 eggs, well-beaten
1 16-oz. can tamales, halved
½ cup grated processed cheese

In a bowl mix two corns, chilis and onion. Pour beaten eggs into bowl, stir into mixture. Put mixture in a metal baking dish. Place tamale pieces on top. Sprinkle with cheese. Cover baking dish with a metal cover, or with foil which is tied down to keep in place. Put metal rack or trivet in slow-cooking pot. Place baking dish on rack. Pour 2 cups hot water into pot. Cover pot. Cook on low 5 to 7 hours, or on high 2½ to 3½ hours.

SUMMER SQUASH AND ORANGES

2 lbs. summer squash
½ tsp salt
1 Tbsp butter or margarine
1 11-oz. can mandarin oranges
2 tsp brown sugar
¼ tsp ground nutmeg (optional)
¼ cup toasted almond slivers
    (optional)

Do not peel squash. Wash squash. Cut into slices, crosswise. Place in slow-cooking pot, add water to come almost to tops of squash. Add salt. Cover pot. Cook on low 6 hours, or on high 3 hours. When done, drain the liquid into a saucepan on top of your stove. In that pan pour syrup from can of oranges. Add sugar. Bring ingredients in saucepan to a boil. Remove from stove, and add to pan the orange wedges and nutmeg (if used). Pour over the squash in the slow-cooking pot. Stir well; remove from pot and serve. Sprinkle with nuts in serving dish.

STEWED RHUBARB

While this is a vegetable, it is included in Chapter 11 in the recipes in the Dessert section.

CHAPTER 11

BEANS, RICE, PASTA RECIPES

When a recipe for the slow-cooking method includes cooked rice or noodles or beans to be served as an accompaniment to the dish, it is best to separately, in a saucepan on the stove, boil them and drain and have them ready for serving. If you need to do this at the last moment, you might avail yourself of the packaged instant-cooking rice and the flaked or powdered potatoes to be mashed, and follow directions on the package. Long-grain converted rice is preferred when the rice is being cooked in slow-cooking pot, although you may use whichever you desire.

BAKED BEANS

3 cups dry navy beans
9 cups water
3 tsp salt
½ cup onions, chopped
½ lb. salt pork, cut in 1-inch
   cubes
¼ cup molasses
1 cup ketchup
¼ cup brown sugar
2 tsp dry mustard

Wash the beans, pick over and discard any not useable. Place beans and all other ingredients in slow-cooking pot. Cover pot. Cook on low 13 to 15 hours, or you may want to test to see when beans are done. (If you need to save cooking time, soak overnight the beans in water to cover. The next day drain water from beans, and proceed as herein directed. Cooking time for slow-cooking pot may be reduced to 8 to 10 hours.)

BAKED BEANS AND PINEAPPLE

½ lb. bacon, diced
2 medium onions, peeled, chopped
2 18-oz. jars or cans baked navy beans
1½ tsp dry mustard
1 9-oz. crushed pineapple
¼ cup chili sauce
¼ tsp salt

In skillet on top of oven, slowly cook bacon and onion. Drain off fat. Place bacon and onion mixture with all other ingredients in slow-cooking pot. Stir to mix well. Cover pot. Cook on low 6 to 8 hours, or on high 3 to 4 hours.

MEDLEY OF SWEET & SOUR BEANS

4 slices bacon
1 onion, peeled, chopped
1 garlic clove, peeled, crushed
1 tsp prepared mustard
¼ cup brown sugar
1 tsp salt
¼ cup vinegar
1 16-oz. can kidney beans, drained
1 16-oz. can lima beans, drained
1 16-oz. can baked beans, drained

In skillet on top of stove, brown the bacon slices. Remove bacon and crumble. In a bowl mix 2 Tbsp bacon drippings from the skillet and all other ingredients excepting the beans. Put mixture in slow-cooking pot. Add beans. Stir to mix well. Cover pot. Cook on low 6 to 8 hours, or on high 3 to 4 hours.

BAKED KIDNEY BEANS

1 lb. bacon, chopped
4 1-lb. cans kidney beans
2 bunches scallions, chopped
   (head and greens)
1 jar chili sauce
1 small green pepper, seeded,
   chopped
2 Tbsp brown sugar

In a skillet on top of oven, fry bacon pieces to remove excess fat. Drain off fat. In a bowl, mix bacon and other ingredients, excepting brown sugar. Place the mixture in slow-cooking pot. Sprinkle brown sugar on top of the food. Cover pot. Cook on low 8 to 10 hours, or on high 4 to 5 hours.

TANGY LIMA BEANS

1 lb. lima beans (soaked overnight)
1 garlic clove, peeled, minced
1 onion, peeled, chopped
1 Tbsp Worcestershire sauce
1 Tbsp prepared mustard
½ tsp chili powder
1 tsp salt
1 10½-oz. can condensed tomato
   soup, undiluted
2 Tbsp brown sugar
2 Tbsp vinegar
¼ lb. salt pork, cubed

In a bowl mix all ingredients, excepting beans and prok. Put beans in slow-cooking pot. Add mixture from bowl. Stir well to mix. Put pork on top of mixture. Cover pot. Cook on low 8 to 10 hours, or on high 4 to 5 hours.

BLACK-EYED PEAS

While these are called peas, actually they are in the same cooking category as beans.

½ lb. bacon or salt pork, chopped
1 lb. dried black-eyed peas (soak
overnight)
4 cups water
1 large onion, peeled, chopped
coarsely
1 1-lb. can tomatoes
2 garlic cloves, peeled, minced
1 tsp dry crushed red pepper (or
2 tsp chili powder)
2 tsp salt
Cooked rice

In a skillet on top of oven, fry the bacon or pork pieces, to remove excess fat. Drain off fat. Place browned meat pieces and all other ingredients, excepting the rice, in slow-cooking pot. Cover pot. Cook on high 1 to 2 hours, then on low for 8 to 9 hours. Serve on bed of cooked rice, which you have separately prepared.

LIMA BEANS WITH HAM

1 lb. lima beans (soaked overnight)
1 medium onion, peeled, chopped
1 large green pepper, seeded, chopped
1 tsp dry mustard
1 tsp salt
½ tsp pepper
½ lb. ham, diced
1 10½-oz. can condensed tomato soup
1 cup water

Place all ingredients in slow-cooking pot. Stir well to mix. Cover pot. Cook on low 8 to 10 hours, or on high 4 to 5 hours (or until beans are cooked).

CHILI BEANS

1 lb. beef chuck, ground coarsely
2 Tbsp shortening
2 1-lb. cans kidney or pinto beans, drained (or ½ lb. dry beans, soaked overnight)
2 cups water
2 medium onions, peeled, chopped coarsely
1 medium green pepper, seeded, chopped coarsely (optional)
2 garlic cloves, peeled, minced
2 Tbsp chili powder
1½ Tbsp salt
1 tsp pepper
1 tsp cider vinegar (optional)

Place all ingredients, in order they are listed, in slow-cooking pot. Cover pot. If raw beans are used, cook only on low 10 to 12 hours. But if canned beans used, cook on low 10 to 12 hours, or on high 5 to 6 hours.

KIDNEY BEANS WITH SAUSAGE

1 lb. kidney beans (soaked overnight)
2 cups water
1 16-oz. can tomato sauce
1 tsp salt
⅛ tsp pepper
1 Tbsp Worcestershire sauce
¾ lb. smoked sausage links, cut
   in 1-inch slices

Put all ingredients, excepting sausage, in slow-cooking pot. Stir to mix well. Cook on low 8 to 10 hours, or on low 4 to 6 hours. Before last two hours on low, or last hour on high, put sausage slices in pot. Recover pot. Finish cooking time.

SAVORY BEANS WITH GROUND BEEF

1 lb. ground beef
1 small onion, peeled, diced
1 16-oz. can kidney beans,
   drained
2 16-oz. cans pork and beans in
   tomato sauce
1 cup ketchup
2 Tbsp vinegar

In a skillet on top of stove, brown the meat. Drain off excess fat. Put meat and all other ingredients in slow-cooking pot. Stir to mix well. Cover pot. Cook on low 3 to 4 hours, or on high ½ to 2 hours.

CHILE CON CARNE

1 lb. ground beef, separated in
   chunks
1 onion, peeled, chopped
1 16-oz. can tomato sauce
2 16-oz. cans kidney beans,
   drained
1½ tsp chili powder
1 tsp salt
1 tsp Worcestershire sauce
1 bay leaf

In a skillet on top of stove, brown the meat. Drain off excess fat. Put meat and all other ingredients in slow-cooking pot. Stir to mix well. Cover pot. Cook on low 4 to 6 hours, or on high 2 to 3 hours. Remove bay leaf before serving.

RICE CASSEROLE

1½ cups evaporated milk, undi-
    luted
½ cup cooking oil
3 eggs, beaten
2 Tbsp minced onion
1 10-oz. pkge frozen chopped
    spinach, thawed, drained (or 2
    cups fresh parsley leaves,
    minced)
2 tsp salt
1 cup shredded American pro-
    cessed cheese, or other cheese
    you prefer
3 cups cooked rice

In a bowl thoroughly mix the milk, oil and eggs. Add the remaining ingredients, and mix. With some of the same cooking oil, grease the inside of the slow-cooking pot. Place the mixed ingredients in pot. Cover pot. Cook on high 1 hour, then on low 4 to 6 hours.

BASIC COOKED RICE

Rice
Water
Butter or margarine
Salt

Read the directions on the box of rice, and follow the amount of water and salt per cup which the label recommends. Rub the inside of the slow-cooking pot with a light film of butter, to grease it. Place rice, water and salt in pot. Cover pot. Cook on high 1½ to 2½ hours. If you can, it is preferable that you lift the cover and stir it a few times during cooking. (You may keep the rice warm for 2 to 3 hours, before serving, by letting rice remain in the pot with the electric turned off.)

RICE AND CLAMS

¼ cup butter or margarine
1 small onion, peeled, chopped fine
1 stalk celery, chopped fine
1 cup raw rice
2 cups chicken broth (or 2 cups water and 2 bouillon cubes)
½ cup grated American processed or other cheese
⅔ cup ripe olives, pitted, chopped
1 7-oz. can minced clams (with liquid)

Place all ingredients in slow-cooking pot. Mix thoroughly. Cover pot. Cook on high 1 hour, then on low 4 to 6 hours.

SPANISH RICE

1½ cups raw rice
½ cup olive oil (or butter or margarine)
1½ cups tomato juice
1½ cups water
1 medium onion, peeled, chopped
1 green pepper, seeded, chopped
1½ tsp salt
1 lb. sausage or ground beef (optional)

If you are going to include the meat, brown it in a skillet on top of the stove to remove excess fat, before including it with the other ingredients in the slow-cooking pot. In a skillet on top of the stove, put the rice and oil, and sauté until rice is golden brown. Place all ingredients in slow-cooking pot. Stir well to mix. Cover pot. Cook on low 4 to 6 hours, or on high 2 to 3 hours.

SPAGHETTI WITH VEGETABLES

1 pkge dry spaghetti mix
1 cup water
1 8-oz. can tomato sauce
1 eggplant, peeled, halved, sliced thin
4 zucchini, cut in ½-inch slices
3 tomatoes, cubed
1 green pepper, seeded, cubed
½ tsp salt
Cooked spaghetti

Put spaghetti mix, water and tomato sauce in slow-cooking pot. Stir to mix. Add other ingredients, excepting spaghetti and cheese. Cover pot. Cook on low 4 to 6 hours, or on high 2 to 3 hours. Serve on a bed of spaghetti, which you have separately prepared. Sprinkle top with cheese.

SPAGHETTI AND BEEF

1 lb. beef, ground
1 Tbsp instant minced onion
1½ tsp salt
½ tsp garlic powder
½ tsp dry mustard (optional)
¼ tsp pepper
¼ tsp. allspice (optional)
¼ tsp mace (optional)
3 cups tomato juice
4 oz. raw spaghetti, broken into
4-inch pieces

In a skillet on top of the oven, brown the ground meat to remove excess fat. Place the meat and all other ingredients, excepting spaghetti, in slow-cooking pot. Stir to mix well. Cover pot. Cook on low 6 to 8 hours, or on high 3½ hours. For the last hour of cooking, keep on high and stir in the spaghetti pieces. Cover pot and continue cooking until spaghetti is done.

NOODLES WITH SPINACH

2 cups cooked noodles (not overcooked)
2 10-oz. pkgs frozen spinach,
1 cup shredded American processed cheese
1 can cream of mushroom soup
½ cup onion, peeled, chopped
⅛ tsp nutmeg (optional)
¼ cup butter or margarine

In a bowl mix all ingredients, stir well. Place mixture in slow-cooking pot. Cover pot. Cook on low 4 to 5 hours, or on high 3 hours. If possible, stir contents in pot several times during cooking.

MACARONI AND CHEESE

4 cups cooked macaroni
2 cups evaporated milk, undilut-
    ed
½ tsp paprika (optional)
1 tsp salt
2 Tbsp minced onion
1 egg, beaten (optional)
2 cups cheese cut into cubes
2 Tbsp butter or margarine

In a bowl mix all ingredients, excepting the macaroni. Stir well. Place the mixture in slow-cooking pot. Cover pot. Cook on high 1 hour, and if possible stir it a few times during that hour. Then add macaroni, and mix it with the sauce in the slow-cooking pot. Cover pot. Cook on low 3 to 5 hours.

COOKED CEREALS

You can prepare your breakfast cereal the night before, and let it cook all night and be ready for you when you get up. While it is usually suggested to use 2 cups of water to 1 cup of cereal, it is best to read directions on the box of cereal and to use the amount of water and salt (in proportion to the cereal) which the food processer recommends.

With butter or margarine, grease the inside of the slow-cooking pot. Place the ingredients in the pot. Cover pot. Cook on low 8 to 10 hours (or overnight).

Cereals suggested for the slow-cooking method are: oatmeal, cornmeal mush, hominy grits, cracked wheat, or whatever you prefer. Do not use "instant" or "quick" cooking cereals in the slow-cooking pot.

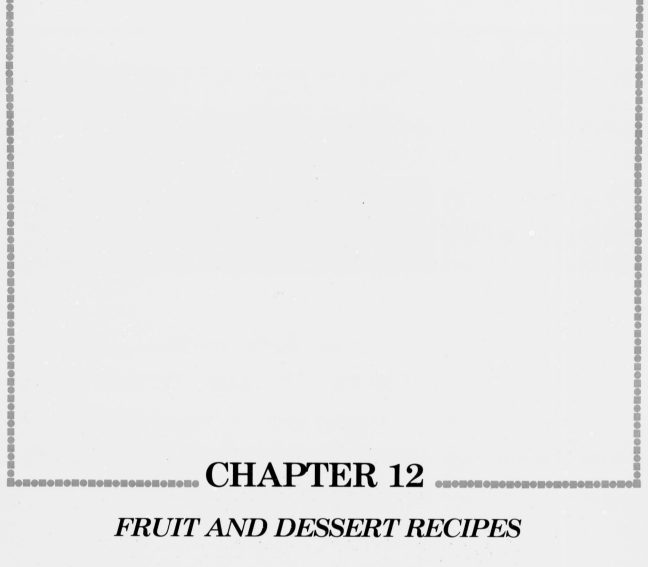

CHAPTER 12

FRUIT AND DESSERT RECIPES

PEARS IN ORANGE SAUCE

3 pears, peeled, halved, pitted
2 cups orange juice
1 cup brown sugar
⅓ cup rum
Sour cream
Sugar mixed with cinnamon
Toasted pecan nuts, chopped

Place pears in slow-cooking pot. Mix orange juice and brown sugar, and pour over the pears. Cover pot. Cook on low 4 hours, or on high 2 hours. Test the pears with a fork to see they are done. About 15 minutes before cooking is done, pour the rum into the pot. Cover pot, and finish cooking. When serving, it is optional to put atop each pear half 1 tbsp sour cream, sprinkle with sugar/cinammon mix and nuts.

123

BAKED APPLES

6 medium baking apples, unpeeled, washed, cored
¼ cup sugar
2 tbsp raisins, seedless
1 tsp cinnamon (optional)
2 Tbsp butter or margarine
½ cup water

In a bowl mix sugar and raisins. Fill the center of apples with this mixture. Sprinkle cinnamon (if you use it) over top of apple, and add a dab of butter. Place apples in slow-cooking pot. Add water. Cover pot. Cook on low 8 hours, or on high 3 hours.

PEARS IN WINE

2 cups dry red wine
2 cups sugar
6 pears, peeled, whole (with
    stems on)
Peel of 1 lemon
Red food coloring (optional)

In a saucepan on top of your stove, place wine and sugar, bring to boil and stir to dissolve sugar. Place pears in slow-cooking pot. Pour wine mix over pears. Add lemon peel and food coloring. Cover pot. Cook on low 4 to 6 hours. When serving, pour the wine sauce over the pears.

CRANBERRY AND APPLE COMPOTE

1 cup cranberries
6 cooking apples, peeled, cored,
    sliced
1 cup sugar
¼ cup port wine
½ cup water
Sour cream

Put cranberries and apple in slow-cooking pot. Sprinkle sugar over fruit. Pour in wine and water. Stir to mix well. Cover pot. Cook on low 4 to 6 hours, or on high 2 to 3 hours. When serving, put sour cream on top (if desired).

CRANBERRY RELISH

1 lb. cranberries
¼ cup water
2 cups sugar

Put all ingredients in slow-cooking pot. Cover pot. Cook on low 4 to 6 hours, or on high 2 to 3 hours. Remove pot cover to see if cranberries have split the skins; if not, cook longer until they do.

COOKED APPLES

8 large cooking apples, peeled,
    cored, cut in chunks or
    crosswise slices
½ cup water
1 tsp cinnamon (optional)
¾ cup sugar

In a bowl mix to a thick consistency the water, cinnamon (if used) and sugar. Place apples in slow-cooking pot. Pour the liquid mixture over apples. Cover pot. Cook on low 8 to 10 hours.

APPLE SAUCE

Follow the preceding cooked apples recipe. When done, press the cooked apple pieces through a food mill or whatever type of strainer you use.

PRUNE AND ORANGE COMPOTE

1 lb. dried prunes, pitted
3 cups water
1 No. 2 can mandarin oranges,
    drained
¼ cup Cointreau (or similar li-
    quer)
¼ cup sugar
½ cup orange juice
2 bananas, sliced

Put prunes and water in slow-cooking pot. Cook on low 2 to 3 hours, or on high 1 to 1½ hours. Remove from pot, put in a bowl, and let cool. Add remaining ingredients, excepting bananas. Put in refrigerator for a few hours. Add sliced bananas before serving.

STEWED PRUNES

1 lb. stewed prunes, pitted
3 unpeeled lemon slices
3 cups water

Put all ingredients in slow-cooking pot. Cover pot. Cook on low 2 to 2½ hours, or on high 1 to 1½ hours.

MIXED FRUIT COMPOTE

1¼ cups dried apricots
1 lb. dried prunes
1 1-lb. can dark cherries, pitted,
 with liquid
1½ cups canned pineapple
 chunks, with liquid
2 cups water

Place all ingredients in slow-cooking pot. Cover pot. Cook on low 7 to 8 hours, or on high 3 to 4 hours.

COOKED DRIED FRUIT

A simple way to cook any dried fruit is to follow the directions on the package of fruit, as to the amount of water to be used in proportion to the amount of fruit. Place fruit and water in slow-cooking pot. Cover pot. Cook on low 7 to 8 hours. This could be served warm or cold, according to your taste; it could be served plain or with a dab of sour cream or some light cream.

STEWED RHUBARB AND STRAWBERRIES

1½ rhubarb stalks (no root or
 leaf ends), cut in ½-inch slices
⅛ tsp salt
⅔ cup sugar
½ cup water
1 pt strawberries, stemmed,
 halved (optional)

Place all ingredients, excepting the strawberries, in slow-cooking pot. Cover pot. Cook on low 4 to 5 hours. (If you want to include the strawberries, add them to pot 30 minutes before you will remove the rhubarb from pot.) Cover pot. Continue cooking on low until done.

SPICY RHUBARB

1½ lbs. rhubarb stalks (no root
 or leaf ends), cut in 1-inch
 slices
¾ cup sugar
3 whole cloves
1 tsp grated lemon or orange
 peel

Put all ingredients in slow-cooking pot. Cover pot. Cook on low 3 to 4 hours, or on high 1¼ to 2 hours. Before serving remove cloves.

RICE PUDDING

2½ cups cooked rice
1½ cups evaporated milk, undiluted
⅔ cup brown sugar
2 Tbsp butter or margarine,
  softened
3 eggs, beaten
½ tsp grated lemon rind
1½ tsp vanilla
½ cup raisedless (optional)

In a bowl mix all ingredients. Grease (with butter) the inside of slow-cooking pot. Place ingredients in pot. Cover pot. Cook on low 4 to 6 hours, or on high 1 to 2 hours. If possible, occasionally stir contents in slow-cooking pot the first 30 minutes of cooking.

BAKED CUSTARD

2 cups milk, scalded, cooled
  down
3 eggs, lightly beaten
⅓ cup sugar
⅛ tsp salt
1 tsp vanilla
Shredded coconut (optional)
Nutmeg (optional)
1 Tbsp butter or margarine,
melted

In a bowl mix eggs, sugar, salt and vanilla. Pour milk into bowl, and stir. Grease inside of a 1-qt metal baking dish with butter. Pour mixture into baking dish. Sprinkle with coconut or nutmeg, if desired. Cover baking dish with metal cover, or with foil tied around with string. In slow-cooking pot put metal rack or trivet. On top of rack place baking dish. Pour hot water into pot, 1-inch depth. Cover pot. Cook on low 4 to 5 hours, or on high 2 to 2½ hours. Before removing custard, test with a knife inserted into the custard. If it does not come out clean, again put cover or foil on baking dish, and cover slow-cooking pot, and cook a little longer until knife comes out clean.

Courtesy of the Pan American Coffee

PLUM PUDDING

4 slices bread, cut in eighths
1 cup milk
2 eggs, lightly beaten
1 cup brown sugar
¼ cup orange juice
6 oz. suet, put through grinder or
　chopped
1 tsp vanilla
1 cup flour
1 tsp baking soda
½ tsp salt
1 tsp ground cloves
1 tsp ground mace
2 cups raisins, seeded
1 cup cut-up dates, pitted
½ cup chopped walnuts
½ cup mixed candied fruits and
peels, ground
1 Tbsp butter or margarine,
melted

In a bowl soak bread in milk. Add eggs, sugar, orange juice, suet and vanilla. Stir to mix well. In another bowl mix flour, baking soda, salt and spices. To this bowl add nuts and fruits. Mix all together. Add this mixture to bread and milk mixture, and stir to mix well. With butter grease the inside of a 2-qt metal mold. Pour the mixture into the mold. Cover mold with foil, tied with a string to hold it. Put a metal rack or trivet in the slow-cooking pot. Place the mold on rack. Pour water into pot to 1-inch depth. Cover pot. Cook on low 10 to 12 hours, or on high 5 to 6 hours. When done, remove mold from pot. Let stand 15 minutes to cool. Then unmold pudding to serve.

APPLE BROWN BETTY

1 cup dry bread crumbs
¼ cup sugar
½ tsp cinnamon
Juice and rind of 1 lemon
2 Tbsp butter or margarine
3 apples, peeled, cored, sliced
¼ cup melted butter or
   margarine
4 cups water

In a bowl mix bread crumbs, sugar, cinnamon, lemon juice and rind. In a buttered mold or pan place a layer of apple slices, then a layer of the bread crumbs mixture; repeat layers of apples and crumb mixture. Pour melted butter over all. Cover with aluminum foil, tied down with a string. Pour water in slow-cooking pot. Place the mold in the pot. Cover pot. Cook on low 3 to 4 hours, or on high 1 to 1½ hours.

BREAD PUDDING

3 slices bread, cut in cubes
1 Tbsp butter or margarine
½ cup brown sugar
¼ tsp salt
½ tsp cinnamon (optional)
2 eggs, lightly beaten
2 cups hot milk
½ tsp vanilla
½ cup raisins, seedless
½ cup chopped nuts (optional)
4 cups water

In a bowl, mix well all ingredients, excepting water. Place the mixture in a buttered mold: cover the container with aluminum foil. Pour water into slow-cooking pot. Place the foil-covered pan in the pot. Cover pot. Cook on low 3 to 4 hours, or on high 1 to 1½ hours.

CHAPTER 13

BREAD AND CAKE RECIPES

BOSTON BROWN BREAD

1 cup white flour
1 cup finely-ground cornmeal
1 cup whole wheat or Graham
  flour
2 tsp baking soda
1 tsp salt
2 Tbsp butter or margarine
½ cup raisins, seeded, or ½ cup
  dates, pitted, chopped (optional)
¾ cup molasses
2 cups buttermilk
2 cups hot water
1 Tbsp butter or margarine,
  melted

In a bowl mix all dry ingredients. Add raisins or dates (if you want to include them). Add molasses and buttermilk. Beat well to form a smooth batter. With melted butter grease inside of 2 1-lb. coffee cans. Pour bread mixture into cans. Cover the cans with aluminum foil, tied around with a string. In slow-cooking pot place a metal rack or trivet. Set the cans on top of the rack. Pour water into slow-cooking pot. Cover pot. Cook on low 4 to 6 hours, or on high 2 to 3 hours. (As there should be water in the slow-cooking pot at all times, it is good to check this and add more hot water if necessary.) When done, turn bread out on a rack to cool.

GINGERBREAD

1 14-oz. pkge gingerbread mix
¼ cup yellow cornmeal
1 tsp salt
1½ cups milk
½ cup raisins, seeded
1 Tbsp butter or margarine,
  melted
Flour

In a bowl mix the gingerbread mix, cornmeal and salt. Stir milk into mixture. Put into electric mixer and beat for 2 minutes at medium speed. Stir raisins into mix. With butter grease inside a 7-cup metal mold, sprinkle flour over greased surface. Pour bread mixture into mold. Cover with foil, and tie it down with a string. Put a metal rack or trivet in the slow-cooking pot. Pour water into pot. Place mold on rack. Cover pot. Cook on low 6 to 8 hours, or on high 3 to 4 hours. Remove mold from pot. Let stand on rack 10 minutes to cool. To take out of mold, slide a knife around the edges to loosen the bread. Turn it out on rack to cool, or it may be served warm.

DATE AND NUT BREAD

1½ cups chopped dates
1½ cups boiling water
1 egg
½ tsp salt
2 tsp faking soda
1 tsp vanilla
1 Tbsp butter or margarine,
  melted
1 cup chopped walnuts
2½ cups flour
1 Tbsp butter or margarine,
  melted

In a bowl place the dates and pour water over them. Let stand 10 minutes. Into the bowl put other ingredients, excepting walnuts and flour, and stir to mix well. In another bowl mix nuts and flour, then stir into date mixture. With melted butter grease the inside of a 1-lb. coffee can or an 8-cup metal mold. Into container pour the bread mixture. Cover top with aluminum foil, then tie with string. Place metal rack or trivet in slow-cooking pot. On this rack place the can or mold. Pour 2 cups hot water into pot. Cover pot. Cook on low 6 to 8 hours, or on high 3 to 4 hours. When done, turn out bread on cooling rack. Serve cool or warm, as you prefer.

APPLESAUCE CAKE

½ cup butter or margarine,
  slightly melted
1 cup brown sugar
1 cup canned (or freshly cooked)
  apple sauce
2½ cups flour
½ tsp baking soda
½ tsp salt
1 tsp baking powder
½ tsp cinnamon
½ tsp ground cloves
¼ tsp nutmeg (optional)
¼ tsp allspice (optional)
1 cup chopped walnuts

In a bowl gradually add sugar to the creamed butter; thoroughly mix it until it is fluffy. Add the apple sauce. Sift together all dry ingredients, then add those to the mixture. Add the nuts, and stir well. As a container, use a metal loaf pan in which you have first placed a sheet of buttered wax paper to line it. Pour the cake mixture into the loaf pan. Do not put a cover on the pan. Place a metal rack or trivet at the bottom of the slow-cooking pot. On top of the rack, place the pan with the cake mixture. Cover the slow-cooking pot. Cook on slow 4 hours, then on high 1 hour. (This recipe is good for 10 portions of cake.)

APPLE CAKE

2 cups sugar
1 cup oil
2 eggs
2 tsp vanilla
2 cups flour
1 tsp salt
1 tsp baking soda
1 tsp nutmeg (optional)
2 cups chopped apples, cored,
  (but not peeled)
1 cup walnuts, chopped
1 Tbsp butter or margarine,
  melted

In a bowl thoroughly beat sugar, oil and eggs. Add vanilla. Sift together the flour, salt, baking soda and nutmeg. To the sugar and eggs mixture add chopped apples. Then add the flour mixture and the chopped nuts. Thoroughly mix all into a smooth batter. Prepare a 2-lb. coffee can or a mold by greasing the inside of it with butter. Into the can pour the mixture. Cover top of can or mold with aluminum foil. Place a metal rack or trivet in bottom of slow-cooking pot. Set the can on the rack. Cover pot. Cook on low 6 to 8 hours or on high 3 to 4 hours.

POUND CAKE

1 16-oz. pkge pound cake mix
2 eggs
⅔ cup water
1 Tbsp butter or margarine,
  melted
Flour

Put into electric mixing bowl the cake mix, eggs and water. Mix at low speed until moistened, then at medium speed for 3 minutes. With melted butter grease inside of an 8-cup mold, then dust flour over the grease. Put cake mix into mold. Cover top of mold with 5 paper towels. Cover slow-cooking pot. Cook on low 5 to 7 hours, or on high 2½ to 3½ hours. To test cake for doneness, insert a toothpick into center of cake, and it should come out clean, even though the top of the cake is moist. When done, remove cake from mold and set it on a rack to cool.

BANANA-NUT CAKE

1 1-lb. pkg yellow cake mix
⅛ tsp baking soda
2 eggs
1 cup water
2 medium bananas, mashed
½ cup chopped walnuts
1 Tbsp butter or margarine,
  melted
Flour

In a bowl put cake mix and baking soda, and stir well. To the bowl add the eggs, water and banana mash. Put into electric mixer all ingredients, excepting nuts, and blend at medium speed for 4 minutes. Add nuts to cake mixture, and stir them in. With melted butter grease the inside of a 2-qt mold, then dust flour over grease. Put cake mixture into mold. Put mold in slow-cooking pot. Cover mold with 5 paper towels. Cover pot. Cook on low 4 to 6 hours, or on high 2 to 3 hours. When done, turn out cake on a rack to cool.

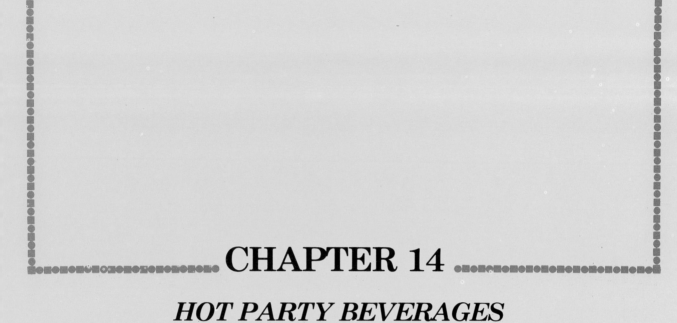

CHAPTER 14

HOT PARTY BEVERAGES

These recipes may be made in proportionately larger or smaller quantities, depending on how many guests will partake of the refreshments.

WASSAIL PUNCH

3 qts apple juice, unsweetened
   (or apple cider)
1 cup sugar
1 6-oz. can frozen lemon juice
   concentrate
1 6-oz. can frozen orange juice
   concentrate
6 cloves, whole
4 cinnamon sticks
1 Tbsp nutmeg, ground
½ cup rum
2 Tbsp cognac

Place sugar, lemon juice and orange juice in slow-cooking pot. In a piece of cheesecloth tie the cloves and cinnamon sticks. Place them, and the nutmeg, into slow-cooking pot. Stir well to mix in the pot. Cover pot. Cook on low 5 hours. Approximately 15 minutes before serving, remove the spice bag from the pot, add the rum and cognac to the pot, and stir. Serving may be done directly from the pot into mugs or punch glasses or the punch may be poured into a punch bowl and served from there. (If you want to add glamor to the serving, about 30 minutes before the punch will be ready in the slow-cooking pot, separately bake in your regular oven, at 350° F., 2 or 3 small oranges or apples, into each of which you have pushed 6 whole cloves, for decoration and for taste. Float this fruit on top of the punch bowl.)

CRANBERRY-PINEAPPLE PUNCH

5 cinnamon sticks, broken in
   half
¾ Tbsp allspice
1½ Tbsp whole cloves
¾ cup brown sugar
3 cups water
⅛ tsp salt
3 cups cranberry juice
3 cups pineapple juice
Orange slices, unpeeled, stud-
   ded with whole cloves

In a cheesecloth bag tie the cinnamon sticks, cloves and allspice. Place spice bag and other ingredients, excepting orange slices, in slow-cooking pot. Cover pot. Cook on low 3 hours. Remove spice bag from pot. Cover pot. Cook on low an additional 3 hours. Serve punch directly from the pot into mugs or punch glasses, or serve from a punch bowl. Garnish the punch with the clove-studded orange slices.

BUTTERED RUM

2½ cups rum
2 qts hot water
2 cups brown sugar
½ cup butter
Pinch of salt
½ tsp ground nutmeg
3 cinnamon sticks
6 whole cloves

Place all ingredients in slow-cooking pot. Stir to mix well. Cover pot. Cook on high 2 hours, then on low 3 to 7 hours. Before serving, warm the drinking mugs. Serve beverage directly from pot into mugs.

MULLED WINE

2/5ths Burgundy, port, claret or
   sweet Sherry wine
1 orange, unpeeled, sliced
2 lemons, unpeeled, sliced
¾ cup sugar
3 sticks cinnamon
1 tsp allspice, whole
20 cloves, whole
½ cup fresh lemon juice

Place all ingredients in slow-cooking pot. Stir to mix well. Cover pot. Cook on low 4 hours, or on high 2 hours.

MULLED CIDER

2 qts apple cider
½ cup brown sugar
2 sticks cinnamon
1½ tsp cloves, whole
1 tsp allspice, whole
Orange slices, unpeeled

In a cheesecloth bag tie the cinnamon, cloves and allspice. Place spices and all ingredients in slow-cooking pot. Cover pot. Cook on low 2 to 7 hours. Remove spice bag. Serve directly from pot into mugs.

CIDER AND ORANGE PUNCH

1 qt apple cider
1 6-oz. can frozen orange juice,
   partially thawed
2 cups water
5 whole cloves
1 tsp nutmeg, ground
2 cinnamon sticks
1 large orange, unpeeled, seeded, sliced thin

Put all ingredients, excepting orange slices, in slow-cooking pot. Cover pot. Heat on low 4 to 6 hours, or on high 2 to 3 hours. Before serving, put orange slices into punch.